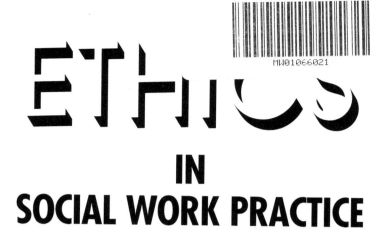

ETHICS
IN
SOCIAL WORK PRACTICE

Edited by
Sonia L. Abels

NARRATIVES FOR
PROFESSIONAL HELPING

LOVE PUBLISHING COMPANY
Denver • London • Sydney

Published by Love Publishing Company
Denver, Colorado 80222

Library of Congress Catalog Card Number 00-104335

Copyright ® 2001 Love Publishing Company
Printed in the United States of America
ISBN 0-89108-285-9

TABLE OF CONTENTS

INTRODUCTION
ETHICAL SENSITIVITY:
A BASE FOR REASONING

Ethic: "A set of moral principles . . .
the moral principles by which any particular person
is guided, the rules of conduct recognized in a
particular profession or area of human life."
(*New Shorter Oxford Dictionary*, 1993, p.856).

BEGINNINGS

From the beginning of their careers, most professional helpers know they have embarked on a moral undertaking. The purpose of this book is to present their voices as they engage in the struggle to make sense of their experiences in ambiguously moral and ethical contexts. Each narrator presents a professional/personal story reflecting the human drama of choosing what's right, as best it can be known. The stories offer different faces of ethical meaning, such as:

- To be an ethical social work leader and academician and thereby risk professional favor
- To violate an institutional policy to protect clients from harm
- To aid a family by trying to prevent the surgeons of a religious hospital from

1

saving the life of the husband/father who had attempted suicide.
- To be a whistle-blower in a foreign country
- To confront an ethical dilemma of treatment cost versus treatment benefit in the end-of-life decision
- To offer a perspective on how power subjugates knowledge
- To forgive those who killed your child by working to improve civil life.

Putting this book together heightened my mindfulness of the relationships between the stories in this collection, and how narratives are used to strengthen ethical reasoning and effect social change. For example, the *New York Times*, in April 2000, printed a series of articles about rage murders in the United States. The investigating reporters built a database from interviews and life histories they collected, comparing the differences and similarities in the murderers. Gruesome, yes, but the data analysis revealed strong correlations with mental illness, the lack of treatment, and professionals and others not recognizing or paying attention to the signals or symptoms the murderers actively displayed. The *Times'* stories, and the database they created, might promote adequate mental health services and create structures that give more purposeful attention to those who seem to be in a dissembling state.

Social work ethics is indeed a serious concern. On the front page of the *Los Angeles Times* (May 3, 2000, p. 1) Kaiser Permanente, one of the largest Health Maintenance Organizations (HMOs) in the United States, announced that psychiatrists must rely on their own examination of patients before prescribing drugs, "rather than on the observations of non-medical psychotherapists, such as social workers and social work interns." The American Psychiatric Association (APA) has launched an investigation, including allegations that in some cases non-medical personnel recommended drugs that could have harmed patients. Some social workers are alleged to have recommended drugs, perhaps under the categories for treatment described in the *Diagnostic and Statistical Manual* (DSM).

> Kaiser's controversial policy came to light in a lawsuit filed . . . by a former Kaiser psychiatrist . . . fired after only a few weeks on the job for refusing to prescribe medication for patients whom he did not personally examine.

Are social workers ethical in offering diagnoses or assessments for psychiatrists' prescribing drugs for the social worker's client? Social workers were following Kaiser's policy, and presumably believed their clients were in need of psychiatric care. Certainly, cost issues affected Kaiser's policy; psychiatric time is more expensive than social-work time. Should social workers ever tell clients that drugs are available to help them? Prescribing drugs is not a purpose, function, or responsibility of social workers. But should social workers recommend drugs be ordered for clients based upon their professional diagnosis?

In California, Kaiser is among the largest employers of social workers. What should the social workers have done? The policy reversal came as state regulators and the APA targeted Kaiser for allegedly violating longstanding medical procedures ("State Law and the APA's Code of Ethics require that physicians conduct an appropriate medical exam of a patient before prescribing drugs.") What should the ethical position of California's National Association of Social Work (NASW) be? And should it take some action?

The code states:

> (d) Social workers should not allow an employing organization's policies, procedures, regulations, or administrative orders to interfere with their ethical practice of social work. Social workers should take reasonable steps to ensure that their employing organizations' practices are consistent with the NASW Code of Ethics.

The psychiatrists relied on social workers and their students' observations of clients to determine if the client required drugs. Clearly, the psychiatrists and the HMO are inherently responsible for the situation. The question we end up with, then, is: What is the profession's and the social workers' ethical responsibility?

NASW frequently challenges proposed state and national legislation and administrative law that seem to violate the profession's Code of Ethics. For example, in February 2000, it took sharp exception to the privacy regulations for electronically stored medical records (including health and mental records of clients) proposed by U. S. Department of Health and Human Services. NASW's concern is that "the proposed regulations would abandon the requirement for clients' written authorization for release of electronically stored mental health."

ETHICS: A DATABASE

Along with other helping professions, social work created a code of ethics to guide its members' behavior as it developed into a profession.

A code is one measure of a profession; it sets out the rules for professional conduct. And the meaning of being a professional has much to do with seeking to live an ethical life.

Over the years the profession has developed sanctions for ethical violations. When a social worker is charged with an ethical violation, the situation is taken before the Committee on Inquiry established by NASW chapters in each state. The inquiry committees become active only when a charge is made and determined valid. To my knowledge, the committees do not make public the reasoning used in the decision making, the ethical principle, the opinion(s) of the board members, the precedents, the reasoning, or the vote.

The methodological history of social work in ethical reasoning seems to be underdeveloped. A database, such as the *New York Times* created, might aid the profession in its ethical decisions and increase public confidence in social-work practice. In most literature on ethics, the concepts discussed are general, composed of a piece from this case and another. They are not real cases that can be used to develop knowledge about ethical reasoning. Rather, they usually are developed for teaching purposes or to make a point about an ethical issue.

Ethics within the profession seem unsettled, and unsettling. Frequently in ethical decisions, there is no certainty of right or wrong. Life is too complicated, with many variables. Ethical uncertainty exists around boundaries, confidentiality, organizational policy, termination, child welfare, juvenile and criminal justice, emotional distress, aging, bioethics, physical and mental health, technology, spirituality, and, most recently, therapy on the Internet (*New York Times*, April 22, 2000). As the Internet embraces daily life, new ethical issues will face us. Doing our best will require more and better data.

METHODOLOGIES FOR ETHICAL REASONING

Upon first review, some of the narratives in this book stirred up competing views of "truth" of the narrator's action. By truth, we mean, here, moral and ethical behavior. As editor of *Reflections*, I believed that the different set of perspectives warranted discourse and engagement with other personal/professional opinions about the "truth" of the narrator's decisions. After publication, conflict again surfaced, with readers passionately expressing significant disagreement over the unintended and intended outcomes.

Conflict frequently arises among reasonable individuals about what is right or moral. The U. S. Supreme Court is the final arbitrator on significant moral issues within the U. S. In both the Warren and Rehnquist Courts, the justices' decisions on social issues of constitutional importance often have been split, five to four, six to three, and even eight to one. In March of 2000, the Court announced a number of important decisions. In one, the Court heard the *U. S. Food and Drug Administration v. Brown and Williamson Tobacco Corporation* petition, seeking legal jurisdiction over tobacco; the FDA argued that tobacco was a drug. The decision was 5 to 4, rejecting the petition (March 21, 2000). And in the petition for a new trial by a convicted murderer scheduled for execution, the justices voted 6 to 3 in favor of a new trial (April 2000).

One could argue that the Supreme Court decisions are legal and not ethical/moral decisions. I argue that Supreme Court decisions are issues of social justice and morality. Among the important concepts is that reasonable persons disagree, even at the highest levels of justice. Although interpretation of the principles of the Constitution, framed by the justices' philosophical interpretation, is a central theme in the Court's process, precedent provides a database that influences the decision. The postmodern view would require an analysis of the justices' constitutional interpretation and philosophy shaped by the political and social context and related to issues of power, status, authority, network, ethnicity, educational background, and gender. As another variable, Justice David Hackett Souter noted that his experience on the Court has changed some of his earlier perspectives. Thus, many factors are involved in the court process: hearing the cases, the justices' questions, and the influence of the justices upon each other.

I believe the Supreme Court inquiry mode is an excellent process for ethical reasoning. The social work profession could follow the lead in creating a database of cases that deal with the ethical decision experiences of social workers. Case records and precedents could aid the profession in strengthening its ethical decision making.

TECHNOLOGICAL CORRECTNESS

Let us imagine what might happen if the ethical concerns raised in the *Reflections* article, "Do the Right Thing," not only were to have written commentary by invited reactors, but also discussion in chat rooms made up of social workers and other helpers. Additional views and examples would expand the thinking as to the most truthful response. These discussion groups would start to provide the type of database our profession could use in developing its ethical decision-making processes, particularly if the stories on the web were delivered in a structured form. This might be a format similar to one of the following:

- The story or narrative describing what happened from the process
- A description and explanation of the reasoning for the decision
- How and why the decision was made
- Both the benefits and the liabilities of the decision
- Discussion of the variety of sources used, such as colleagues, research, literature
- The principle(s) from the code of ethics they followed, or that guided them
- What actually happened—the outcomes
- The intentional and unintentional consequences.

Although most of the ethical situations are expected to come out of grounded social work practice, some of the commentary might include views of philosophers, medical personnel, lawyers, academicians, and those who are, or have been, clients.

Use of the Internet, of course, presents new ethical concerns. As the Internet continues to grow, a database, using the same mode of inquiry, could aid social work and the helping professions as a whole in responding appropriately to some of the unanticipated issues. As a growing number of helpers are offering services via the Internet, confidentiality may become a central theme. Are there ethical considerations aside from quality-of-service issues? What guidelines does our profession offer? Can group counseling and support groups be held to confidentiality guidelines?

At the actual point of practice, most of us react at a preconscious state of ethical behavior. As the situation unfolds, our ethical reactions are not separate from, but are internal to, practice. Usually we do not seek out the specific ethical principle and its explanation from the professional Code. Only when we have nagging doubt or conflict do we search for other answers. It's when we have intellectual doubt that we seek other opinions and feedback. Sometimes, when people disagree with our opinions, we engage in the search for the right answer, as best as can be known. Social workers' distinguished capability of self-awareness, and its auxiliary, feedback, is a factor in knowing if something is not quite right. Cases from individual social workers and social work ethics boards, with all the variables identified, could create a database.

I propose that the profession begin to develop an empirical base, permitting review of other professional decisions. It might add to the profession's ethical sensitivity as members face particular ethical uncertainty. It also might aid the profession's ability to respond to ethics directly involved in administration, program, and public and agency policies that affect clients adversely.

A public welfare office in a large city created a policy of "strongly recommending" that very young single mothers marry the father of the baby (a man who is frequently older, and had sexually assaulted her). Money was the sanction. The agency severely punished a worker who publicly questioned both the policy and the procedure, and pushed her out of her job. The agency became more secretive. The case was not taken up as an ethical violation. The system and the politics were just too powerful.

CONFIDENTIALITY: YOU CAN'T ALWAYS BANK ON THE PRINCIPLE

The following two anecdotes dealing with issues of confidentiality are presented to illustrate that a principle does not, and cannot, function as a rule in all cases. Although a database would not provide certainty, it would offer additional direction, or tendencies. As a faculty member with some responsibility for student placements, I witnessed the first situation and used the second in my practice class to experiment with a structure of inquiry for resolving ethical conflicts similar to the one suggested earlier in this introduction.

On an agency visit, the field instructor and I were discussing the student's assignment when the phone rang. The supervisor indicated that I should stay. I heard the supervisor's part of the call, and she filled in the rest of the story afterward.

> The agency offers family services and a halfway house for persons returning from the mental hospital, before reentering the community. The phone call was from a barber in the neighborhood. Almost every day for the past year, he had been shaving a person living in the halfway house. He was concerned. They used to kibitz together, and he came to the barbershop for a shave every weekday. It was now Thursday, and the barber hadn't seen the customer since the previous Friday.

The barber knew that the agency ran the halfway house and thought it could tell him how to contact his customer and find out where he was. The supervisor said she was sorry but she could not tell him, as it was a matter of confidentiality and her client had not given permission to the agency to tell anyone. The barber pushed for information, as the man was a friend and he wanted to know how and where he was.

The worker did not know how the man was, as he was back in the mental hospital, and she believed she could not violate the client's confidentiality by telling the barber where he was.

The conversation persisted without resolution. The supervisor told the barber that it was agency policy to maintain their client's confidentiality.

I questioned the decision and made an empathetic statement to the supervisor about the situation. She agreed that it was a tough decision but stated that maintaining confidentiality was crucial in order to keep the community's confidence in the social work staff and in the agency. The situation puzzled me. Would it have been better for the barber to know where the man was, to visit him and to continue his expression of friendship? Would it violate the community's trust if he had been told? And would it have been better for everyone concerned for the barber to know? Of course, the worker might have found a way to contact the mentally distressed man or his worker but he was out of the agency's jurisdiction, and the hospital too, had a policy of confidentiality. The worker could have sent the hospital worker a note, telling about the barber's concern.

I did not express any of my thoughts to the worker. Upon reflection, I believed that might alienate her, that she would not like my disagreeing with her, and so on. Perhaps I was less than moral or ethical. Certainly it might have benefited the barber, and perhaps the client. I now know my decision was wrong. I, too, could have followed up and sent a letter explaining my view—or prepared a paper to present to the agency—with the supervisor's participation to discuss the issue. I believed the focus was the student's learning and that was my function. Was my function also to be an ethical person?

Confidentiality certainly is an ethical issue. The Code of Social Work Ethics makes clear that client confidentiality is uppermost and can be violated only under specific circumstances, usually legal or life-and-death issues. A database of ethical cases could provide more grounded answers on issues including confidentiality. Some narratives presented in this series provide a vigorous discourse about ethical decisions such as this one.

The second situation led to a framework developed at Cleveland State University, after the students and I were confronted with a case about confidentiality (That framework appears in the Appendix).

> A client told the field student intern that she was pregnant and was planning to marry the father of the baby. The student also was working with this client's mother, who had told the student about her own sexual relationship with the same man that her daughter was going to marry. The mother did not want to tell her daughter that she was having a sexual relationship with her daughter's boyfriend.
>
> The student-worker asked the class if she should tell the daughter about her mother. We did not know what was ethically correct. At that point, with the help of the director of the college, we worked out a structure for dealing with ethical conflicts, and then used the data to make a decision.
>
> We proposed that the worker ask the mother to consider telling the daughter about her relationship, and to ask the boyfriend to do the same. Neither agreed. Because the daughter was 18, the agency could not identify a legal violation of sex with minors.
>
> I think the social worker did the best she could have done, and perhaps things worked out over time for the parties involved. Under the expressed conditions, the social worker tried to figure out the right decision. The mother told her boyfriend that she was no longer going to see him.
>
> Did things work out, and did they all live happily ever after? We hoped so, but we decided that it was the mother's issue, and that the worker should not tell the daughter. In a sense, it was also a gender issue. The man knew what he was doing was harmful but had no second thoughts—except he agreed with the mother that once he and her daughter were married, he could no longer have sex with the mother. I suspect that at some point everyone in the family knew what had happened.

Even with the best decision-making process, lives are so complicated that good doesn't necessarily happen. Sometimes the best that can be hoped for is that there is careful reasoning; that all things are considered; that good use is made of available knowledge; and that the situation is given considerable and serious reflective thought. Even experts in ethics do not always recognize the contradictions present in practice.

In the final analysis, however, doing the right thing often entails personal risk. Being ethically sensitive demands that we act when we recognize unethical practices. In 1963, Benny Max Parrish, a social worker for the Alameda County Welfare Department, in California, was dismissed for insubordination for refusing to participate in a mass raid upon the homes of the County's welfare recipients. Parrish sued for reinstatement and the case reached the California Supreme Court. The court upheld Mr. Parrish's position with the following comment: "It is surely not beyond the competence of the department to conduct appropriate investigations without violence to human dignity, and within the confines of the constitution."

Readers of this book have the opportunity to compare their own ethical perspectives with those of the narrators and the commentators. The difficulties present in our work with clients in various contexts require decisions based on ethical sensitivity.

I hope the narratives presented in this series evoke vigorous and interesting discussions. The stories have a grand stature. They are stories of a search for meaning.

HOW I DIDN'T BECOME A PSYCHOTHERAPIST

By Harry Specht

The late Harry Specht was Dean
and Professor, School of
Social Welfare, University
of California, Berkely.

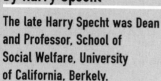

In 1951, when I graduated at age 21 from City College in New York City (CCNY), I had had a good deal of paid experience in social work. But I wanted very much to be a "professional" social worker which meant getting a master's degree. I had met many practitioners in the centers, settlement houses, and camps where I had worked whom I admired and looked up to and who had master's degrees in social work. I was excited, therefore, to be accepted at the School of Applied Social Sciences (SASS) at Western Reserve University in Cleveland, Ohio, as a graduate student majoring in social group work.

I had grown up in the Bronx and had never travelled out of New York City except when I went to camp in upstate New York. I was under the impression that Cleveland was "out west." I was somewhat disappointed when I arrived there to find that it didn't look all that much different from New York City, except that the sign that said "SOCONY" (e.g., Standard Oil Company of New York) in the Bronx was "SOHIO" in Cleveland.

However, SASS was on campus, an idyllic place, and I lived at Roosevelt Co-op which was only a block away. That gave me a sense of being part of campus life that I hadn't had when I attended City College New York. Although downtown Cleveland had a small town quality, it wasn't any more beautiful than New York City. But the campus was beautiful and I enjoyed being in that setting. About one-third of the 20-or-so students living at the co-op were going to SASS and we developed close relationships.

Overall, I loved being at SASS. I thought that the teachers were very good. (Among my teachers were Grace Coyle, Margaret Hartford, and Ray Fischer.) We considered most of them to be very learned and we treated them with respect. As a group they tended to be much more dedicated to service than my colleagues are today. We, as students, wanted to be taken seriously and tried to emulate our teachers in demonstrating our caringness and dedication. Our papers and class discussions often had a slight confessional quality to them because it was considered a good thing to talk about your weaknesses, your desire to integrate learning, and your selflessness, all of which were to be attained by a "conscious use of self."

The curricula content for masters students encouraged this kind of introspection. All students had to take courses in human growth and development. These courses given by psychiatrists delivered undiluted psychoanalytic theory. The practice courses heavily favored psychoanalytic interpretation. A required course called "Medical Information" was also psychoanalytic. There were courses also in social policy (very dry) and community organization (CO). Some psychoanalytic interpretation slipped even into the CO course. Most students, including me, ate up this psychoanalytic stuff with gusto. In our informal social exchanges we never missed an opportunity to joke about "repression," "hostility," and "transference." In the process records we wrote in field work we were expected to demonstrate our capacity to use this material.

In both class and field there was a larger premium placed upon discussion about self and about experiences in practice than was placed on scholarship. I found classes interesting and the assignments mostly easy. I had majored in English at college so writing came fairly easily to me. Although I didn't do a great deal of reading I found that my ability to absorb the little scholarly and theoretical material covered and apply it in written assignments won me more recognition than I'd expected. I was young, working to support myself, and more interested in doing than in scholarly analysis.

I was not especially challenged by my first-year field work assignment with the Jewish Community Centers of Cleveland. By and large, I did passable work with a senior citizens' club (then known as a "Golden Age Club"), a 6th grade boys' group, and a lounge program for young adults. I found most of the work not very challenging because it was similar to work with groups I'd been doing before I went to SASS. Most of my learning that year was stylistic—getting comfortable with professional language, participating in staff meetings, writing process records, and "making use of supervision." I had to stretch and dissemble a bit to do the latter because there wasn't a great deal in my assignments for a somewhat experienced student to learn. However, I was earnest about school and tried hard to "grow" and to "integrate knowledge in practice."

I had one rather jolting experience in Grace Coyle's social group work class in the second semester. At that time Miss Coyle was in her 60's and that seemed to most of us to be old. We thought her to be a scholar/philosopher and treated her reverentially. We also thought she was pretty. Those of us living at the Co-op agreed that if Betty Boop had become an older scholar she would have looked just like Grace Coyle. In her class, students had to make oral presentations on some structural feature of one of the groups with which they were working. I chose to speak about the use of the concept of culture in my work with the senior citizens' group. I explained to the class some of the behavioral differences one finds among Litvak, Galitziana, and Sephardic Jews, how older Jews tend to respond to a young Jewish male, and a few other items. In my presentation, I told some anecdotes that I thought to be amusing and in the telling I made use of a number of Yiddish phrases. Many of my non-Jewish classmates thought I was hilarious and laughed appreciatively; I warmed to my subject and added more humor. My presentation became very jokey. Miss Coyle was not amused. When I concluded she quietly said something like: You are a bright and witty young man; you may even be sensitive; but you will have to work harder to strengthen that aspect of yourself so that it becomes more evident. I was devastated. I felt that I had to redeem myself with Miss Coyle. I decided that my work on the final assignment for the course—a group analysis—had to be one of the great documents of the age. I have never worked so hard on anything I've ever written. My analysis was long. It was stuffed with everything I'd read that year. And it was SENSITIVE, jam-packed with psychoanalytic, cultural, and sociological interpretations. There was a sociogram too. And each section had a little headnote from something I'd read as an English major at college. I even paid a professional typist to do it up for me. To my eyes, it was as splendid a piece of work as I could imagine. In retrospect, I think Miss Coyle must have been vastly amused at the extraordinary effort I had put into this work. She returned my paper with a note of lavish praise. No other review of my work has ever pleased me so much. Miss Coyle probably recognized that I'd put a lot of work into that paper and she decided that I deserved to be taken out of the doghouse.

As a student of Miss Coyle, I wondered what she thought about the heavy dose of psychoanalytic theory we were getting. She taught none of it in her courses. She favored sociological and social psychological theories, and gave a strong emphasis to citizenship education. I noticed that she listened intently when students or other teachers used psychoanalytic theory, but I never heard her make a comment about it. I regret that I hadn't the intellectual initiative or security to question her about it.

In my second year at Western Reserve, I asked to have a field placement in a mental hospital. I was placed at Cleveland Receiving Hospital which had a department called "Therapeutic Group Work." I made this request because of my experiences prior to graduate school. In the late 1940s, Albert Deutsch, a columnist for a liberal New York City newspaper called *PM*, began writing about the terrible treatment of the mentally ill in state hospitals. (Deutsch's book, *The Shame of the States*, published in 1948, was the intellectual cornerstone of the great movement for deinstitutionalization in the 1960s and 1970s.) I was deeply affected by Deutsch's writings because I had a relative and a friend who were institutionalized and I was bothered by how they were treated. Then, in 1951 I read a book called *The Snakepit*, a story about the experiences of a mentally ill woman in a state mental hospital, and saw the 1951 film with Olivia De Havilland which was based on the book. I thought the book and the movie were chilling. I was determined, then, to do something to help the mentally ill. (Of course, I didn't have any notion of how I would help. I think that at that age, just the idea of committing myself to help someone seemed to be, in itself, a significant act.)

The mission of the staff of the Department of Therapeutic Group Work was to enable patients to make use of their social resources and other resources of the hospital to help them regain health. The group workers did not do psychotherapy with individuals or with groups. After some initial anxiety over being in intimate contact with seriously mentally ill people, I was comfortable working in that setting and found I could make excellent use of my knowledge and skills. The interaction with other professionals—nurses, doctors, psychologists—was intellectually stimulating. I felt I was doing something important and useful.

To work in that setting, it was necessary to read a lot of material on psychiatry to learn the nomenclature and aetiology of mental illness. I read a good deal of psychoanalytic material which I found interesting and compelling. Psychoanalytic theory is dramatic; psychoanalysis relies heavily on interpretations of the symbolism in personal behavior, interpersonal interactions, and dreams. I enjoyed it. I found psychoanalytic theory to be very readable and easily applicable in interpreting all kinds of personal behavior. (I think, too, that psychoanalytic theory gives one a sense of power over others. That is, in using ideas about, for example, the unconscious, psychosexual development, and mechanisms of defense, you come to believe that you are party to secrets about others of which they themselves are unaware.)

My experiences in that placement left me wanting to continue working with the mentally ill. I was thrilled, then, to be hired for a residential position at Ittleson Center in New York City. Ittleson Center served hospitalized mentally ill adolescents. It was under the direction of David Wineman who was a collaborator of the well-known Fritz Redl. (Redl and Wineman published a book called *Children Who Hate* [Free Press, 1951] which I found gripping, creative and useful.) However, when I arrived in New York City I learned that there was no job for me at Ittleson Center because David Wineman had been fired. Apparently, one of the reasons he had been fired was that he'd hired me, a social group worker, instead of a more clinically oriented professional.

Wineman's departure from Ittleson left me in New York City without a place to live (I had expected to reside at Ittleson), without a job, and little money. It was in September, so most jobs in social group work had been filled because group work agencies follow an academic year. A position was open at Lenox Hill Neighborhood Association, a settlement house on the east side of mid-Manhattan. Lenox Hill was desperate to hire a worker who would work with youth gangs. Donors had provided funds for this program and Lenox Hill was eager to have something tangible to show them. They had been counting on Irving Spergle to take the position but he'd taken a teaching job at the University of Chicago. (Spergle became one of the nation's foremost authorities on gangs and juvenile delinquency.) I wasn't the kind of worker they'd been hoping for. Irving Spergle was certainly better suited for the position than I was. And Lenox Hill was not the situation I'd been hoping for. But neither Lenox Hill nor I had many choices, so I took the job.

There were three parts to my job. First, I became the group leader of the "Raiders," a group of teenagers and young adults who were considered to be a "gang." Second, I was responsible for a holiday program for the children of working parents. This involved organization of an all-day program for scores of these children on school holidays. And third, I was to assist in supervising the after-school program for grade school children. I was clearly unprepared for the first two assignments. I found the Raiders intimidating. They were big, tough, athletic, and, to me, threatening. I was thin, delicate, and unathletic. I knew little about the problems of working parents and the kinds of social resources they needed. However, I had the good fortune to be supervised by an outstanding professional, Victor Remer. Vic was a big, athletic, and extremely sensitive man with many years of experience working with difficult teenagers and in poor neighborhoods. He was interested in and, I think, entertained by my psychoanalytic orientation. Conversant with psychoanalytic theory, he never put it down. He seemed to know exactly how uncomfortable I was in dealing with the Raiders. With great skill he helped me discover how I could respond to their disruptive, posturing, and testing behavior. I was surprised to find that I could set limits for these young men, that they wanted me to help them grow up, and that there were many ways I could help them. I also learned a great deal from Vic about utilizing social services and community groups to help families. Within a couple of months I believed that I had been very lucky to get the job at Lenox Hill.

I continued to work in community centers and residential camps with groups and adult organizations for several years. Gradually, I developed an interest in the ideas and theories that underlaid the work

I was doing. This began with a problem in work with teenage groups that nagged me. It seemed to me that many social group workers tended to be excessively permissive in work with teenagers to a point that they provided insufficient guidance and structure in developing programs with group members. This resulted in the first paper I ever published called, "A Program Curriculum for Social Club Groups" (*Journal of Jewish Communal Services,* Winter, 1957). It is not a very good paper from a scholarly point of view, but it did strike upon a sensitive issue among social group workers and resulted in some discussion in professional meetings. In those years, I began to read more about theory and social policy issues. Up until then, my intellectual interests had centered around practice.

In 1960 I was accepted at Brandeis University's Florence Heller School for Advanced Studies in Social Welfare. Brandeis was a new school which took the study of social policy as its central mission, and fit my developing interests. My goals in doctoral study hadn't crystallized any further than that vague idea. Mostly, I thought it would be elevating both intellectually and professionally to have a Ph.D. Consequently, I was not a very good doctoral student because I lacked the focus that advanced studies requires. However, I did manage to complete the program. The major benefits it had for me were to increase my understanding of research methodology and to improve my writing skills.

After completing the program at Brandeis I worked for two years at Mobilization for Youth (MFY) in New York City as director of the community organization program and then for two years in Richmond, California, in community organization. MFY was a massive project to prevent juvenile delinquency, the predecessor to the national War on Poverty in the 1960s. It constituted an intellectually challenging experience because it was a planned effort to test the theories put forward by Richard Cloward and Lloyd Ohlin in their book, *Delinquency and Opportunity.* I left MFY for the job in Richmond for two reasons. First, my wife and I wanted to move to the San Francisco Bay Area. Second, the Richmond job gave me an opportunity to test out some of my own ideas in practice.

The programs in Richmond involved a primarily African-American constituency. Between 1964 and 1966 it became difficult for a White organizer to take a leadership role in a Black community. The civil rights movement had begun to change the relationships between Whites and Blacks. There was, nationally, a rejection by African-American activists of their long-standing dependency on White leadership, and there was a militant call for "Black Power." From the point of view of Black community development, this was a good thing. But personally it was painful for many of us—both Whites and Blacks—associated with the movement.

I took a job as a teacher, for one year at the Department of Social Work at San Francisco State University, and then, in 1967, at the School of Social Welfare, University of California at Berkeley. For about 15 years I did research on and wrote about community organization, social planning, and social policy. These were not the subject matters that had brought me into social work. But there was, in that period, a burgeoning excitement about civil rights, the War on Poverty, and the Model Cities Program. My colleagues, George Brager from Mobilization for Youth and Ralph Kramer at Berkeley, both of whom had plied those scholarly furrows for many years, got me writing on the subject. Brager and Kramer two original thinkers developed a theoretical perspective on community organization that was new, enlarging the intellectual boundaries of practice. The field—especially the part concerned with grassroots organizing—was relatively new, so it was easy to publish almost anything about it. Somewhat later, another colleague, Neil Gilbert, drew me into a collaboration on social policy that lasted a decade. The study of social policy was even more far afield from my original interest because it has, relatively, little connection to practice. It is a more intellectual line of thought and draws heavily upon economics, law, political science, and organization theory. The study of social policy broadened my thinking a lot. Neil Gilbert has a sharp and creative mind and working with him forced me to be clearer and more rational in my work.

In 1977, I became dean of the School of Social Welfare at Berkeley. As a professor I had been attentive primarily to my interests in community organization, social planning, and social policy. As dean, I became interested in the whole enterprise of social work education. The vast majority of our students were studying for careers in direct practice, and I didn't know very much about their studies and their field work.

I began sitting in on courses in case work (now called "direct practice") and reading material from course outlines. The content of these courses was not based on a strictly psychoanalytic framework as it had been 25 years before when I'd gone off to take a job at Ittleson Center. There was still some of it, most representative in the work of Erik Erikson. In addition there were some elements of behavior modification techniques and social learning theory (e.g., Bandura, Gambrill, and S.D. Rose), and large elements of humanistic psychology (e.g., C. Rogers, A. Maslow, and V.S. Sexton).

I was taken aback by the great lack of substance in this material. The behavior modification material is atheoretical. These scholars deal with techniques for modifying behavior. They are super-scientific and deal only with what can be measured. As a consequence, they tend to deal best with very teensy-weensy problems, for example phobias. They do not, as far as I can see, have an interest in larger social problems—e.g., poverty, alienation, loneliness—but only in measurable problems that can be seen in the behavior of individuals.

It is the theories from humanistic psychology that are most predominant in education for direct practice. But there isn't a great deal of theory in these humanistic "theories." What there is, though, is a powerful set of attitudes about the innate goodness of human beings, and about the capacity of human beings to grow and change.

I went on to read about research on psychotherapy. The conclusion one must draw from the research is that there is little evidence to support the efficacy of this kind of intervention. There is clear evidence that most people who get psychotherapy like it; and most of them like their psychotherapists. But that is not the same thing as effectiveness in problem solving.

I examined the list of agencies in which our students did their field work. I was astounded to learn that of 200 graduate students only one was doing field work in a public social services department.

Finally, I read all available literature on the careers of professional social workers. It was distressing to learn that social work graduates were going by the droves into the private practice of psychotherapy. Between 1975 and 1985 the number of social workers in private practice had increased fivefold. By 1991, 57% of the members of the National Association of Social Workers were in for-profit practice for at least part of their work week. You do not have to be a genius to conclude from what I had discovered in my studies that something has gone terribly wrong with the profession of social work.

Midway into my explorations of current social work practice, I concluded (mistakenly, I now believe) that one important reason for social work's neglect of its true mission was the lack of useful social theories to guide intervention. I began reading in the field of social psychology and was delighted to find that the field abounds with theories that are exceedingly useful in describing and analyzing social behavior. (This is in contradistinction to psychological and psychoanalytic theories which analyze individual behavior.) I'm referring to such theories as social exchange theory, attribution theory, theories of interpersonal relationships, and social network analysis. Over the last 50 years, social psychology has developed a set of theories that are right on the button for social work practice; these theories have been almost entirely ignored by social workers.

In the course of my career I had written frequently about controversial issues in social work and social welfare. These controversies usually revolved around issues of ideology (e.g., "The Deprofessionalization of Social Work," *Social Work,* March 1972) or pedagogy (e.g., "Undergraduate Education and Professional Achievements of MSWs" (with Britt and Frost, *Social Work,* May 1984). The issue of psychotherapy was different. It was something I had to struggle with personally and intellectually. Although I had never engaged in that sort of practice, like most other people in our field—indeed, like most other Americans—I had been nurtured and socialized with the radical individualism of scholars such as Freud, Rogers, and Maslow. It was extremely difficult to shake loose from the intrapersonal orientations I had integrated since I was an older teenager. At first, I found it difficult to utilize such social psychological theories as, for example, social exchange theory, social network analysis, and attribution theory. Only gradually was I able to shift from a focus on the intrapersonal and grasp the importance of analyzing the interpersonal aspects of practice. These studies led me to write a book about social work practice, *New Directions in Social Work Practice* (Prentice-Hall, 1988). In this volume, I introduce readers to these social psychological ways of thinking. In addition, I attempt to distinguish between the functions of social workers and the functions of psychotherapists. I think it is a good book, but it has had no significant impact. I realized from this experience (rather late in life, I think) that a good idea is not necessarily a good enough reason for people to change. After all, why should practitioners and teachers change their way of thinking if they are already established in a career that has provided them with position, status, and tangible rewards? I came to believe that the profession was not capable of reforming itself. Moreover, it appeared more and more evident to me that the profession's drift to psychotherapy was becoming a floodtide.

For these reasons I wrote the paper, "Social Work and the Popular Psychotherapies," which I submitted to *Social Work* (SW) in 1989. I was puzzled when the article was rejected with comments from two readers that it was filled with "polemic distortions, and bias," that my argument was "one-sided," and that I used "unsubstantiated statements." I was then at a stage in life when the publication of one more paper was not important to my career. And I knew that the paper was relevant, clear, and to the point. It occurred to me that the editors of SW were simply not able to countenance the idea that psychotherapy is not a proper mode of intervention for our profession. So, I sent the paper to *Social Service Review (SSR)* where it was published. *SSR* followed up with two "Debates With Author."

The positive responses to the *SSR* article, and the odd responses I'd gotten from the *SW* readers, made me think that the debate should be pushed further, and I decided to do a book-length treatment of the material in the *SSR* articles and debates. I intended to aim the book at a broad audience, not just social workers. The outcome of that decision is the book (written with Mark Courtney) *Unfaithful Angels: How Social Work Has Abandoned Its Mission* (Free Press, 1994).

I ought to conclude this memoir by pointing up the lessons I have learned in my journey from *SASS* to *Unfaithful Angels,* but I'm not sure what they are. I think I didn't become a psychotherapist because even before graduate school I was attracted by the idea that social interaction (as opposed to intrapersonal examination) can be healing, and that people have a great capacity to help and nurture one another. My earlier experiences in settlement houses and camps had reinforced this notion and I had many fine supervisors and teachers who helped me to think about and refine my ideas. Beyond that, there seems to have been a lot of happenstance and luck (both good and bad) in my making of life choices. As I write it here in retrospect the flow of life events appears to have more rationality and integrity than is the case in reality. The meanings, if there are any, sound like the homely virtues my mother taught: "Be true to yourself"; "Stand up for what you think is right"; "Care about people in need." Those are certainly values to live by, but how each of us perceives and realizes these values is a complex matter.

THE INSURRECTION OF SUBJUGATED KNOWLEDGE

Introduction to "Do the Right Thing"

By Paul Abels and
Sonia Leib Abels

In the following chapters each author's narrative voice explores in depth the dramatic events that occurred as he/she professionally entered other person's lives, engaged in efforts to do the right thing, and confronted the moral complexity of making the "right" decisions. The authors' narratives present an opportunity to initiate a discourse with the reader—to examine and comment on the narrators' practice, and decisions—decisions, some of which were not necessarily prudent, and frequently, at a risk to themselves. Through this public disclosure the power of narratives bursts forth. Our payback to the narrator is an active response to his/her demand—to reexamine both the complexities and the possible consequences of our own practice. As John Kayser suggests, one of the purposes of making public a story about a "private experience," is to help other readers to reflect and compare their own experiences in practice and in teaching. (1996. Written in a manuscript review)

The narrative "Do the Right Thing" challenged the Executive Board of *Reflections* to examine its own value perspectives. Our discourse, difficult and conflictal, generated the idea to invite others to participate to examine the complexities this case presents. We invited five commentators to express their ideas about the events in "Do The Right Thing." All react to issues of law, ethics, morality, class structure, social justice, oppressed clients, organizational authority, "right" decisions, risk, and power. Power on a number of levels, the power of the bureaucracy, the power of the professions to use their resources for social change and social control, and the power of the individual to make decisions that may have retributive consequences.

At the core is the politics of power, the power of persons and institutions to dominate the discourse of knowledge. Foucault in the 1970's and 1980's examined how language influences society's discourse and how those who control language and thus discourse, wield tremendous power. We intellectually realized that which we knew intuitively—the meaning of subjugated knowledge. Foucault spoke of subjugated knowledge as the power to both determine and limit the knowledge certain groups might have access to, or knowledge that many persons are prevented from making public.

Narratives of those without power—marginalized persons—are not listened to. Those with power use language to decide who is insane, a criminal, a deviant, to be ignored or deprived of certain rights. Bruner said that "dominant narratives are units of power as well as meaning. The ability to tell one's story has a political component." Ignored narratives in Foucalt's view is subjugated knowledge. Narratives provide opportunity for an open hearing. Ungar in his review of the film "Lone Star" forcefully uncovers this view when he says ". . . film has become one of the few places where one can find reliable information about meaningful insight into the immigrant experience. While politicians bash immigrants, film makers—and novelists along with them—tell us gripping immigrant stories, recording them before they disappear." *(NY Times)*.

Foucault calls for an: "insurrection of subjugated knowledge," to present opportunities for the powerless to be heard, to provide alternative views of life, to help people see where rules and regulations come from, and whom they serve. In practice, Michael White has attempted to do this in his work with narrative therapy. The attempt is to help people construct the narratives they prefer, rather than the ones they have been led to believe they must adhere to. These range from the narratives of battered women, the poor, the aborigines—to the narratives assigned to the helping professions.

In the first issue of *Reflections,* Jane Gorman in "Being and Doing" tells the story of the uncovering subjugated knowledge in a doctoral class on practice theory ". . . there were . . . a distinguished group, having been directors of various social service agencies. One day . . . I talked about the times I felt like a real social worker . . . and asked about their experiences. One by one students recounted times when, behind the back of the professional role, they went to a client's house with an armful of groceries, sat with a client in court, wept with a client in pain . . . when our dreams of the profession met reality . . . came when we shed our professional hats, just to get an opportunity to be with people was exhilarating and humorously absurd."

Annie Houston's article, "Do The Right Thing," about her work in a corrections facility jars with a stronger dissonance than the incidents described above, yet reveal the same hidden concerns about subjugated knowledge in the helping professions.

We have asked five people from various fields to comment on her article. We would welcome your commentary.

REFERENCES

Bruner, E.M.(1986) Experience and expression, in V.W. Turner and E.M. Bruner. *The anthropology of experience.* Chicago: University of Illinois Press.

Foucault, M. (1980). *Power/Knowledge: Selected interviews and other writings.* 1972–1977. NY: Pantheon.

Ungar, S. J. (June 23, 1996) Immigrants' tales in subtle shades of gray. *New York Times.* H 15, 28.

White, M. (1991) Deconstruction and memory. *Dulwhich Center Newsletter.* 21–40.

DO THE RIGHT THING[1]

3

By Annie L. Houston

Annie L. Houston, LCSW–C was formally Supervisor, Intensive Family Services, Anne Arundel County Department of Social Services, Annapolis, Maryland.

As a beginning graduate social work student intern, I was faced with ethical dilemmas, moral conflicts and decisions that shaped my views about systems, institutions and professional advocacy. This narrative describes my work with incarcerated women who were able to keep their babies with them while they were in prison. My practice, in support of the women's informal system which acted to prevent the spread of HIV and AIDS, I believe was in the women's best interests.

AUTHOR'S NOTE

I wish to acknowledge and thank Dr. Barbara Levy Simon, Associate Professor at the Columbia School of Social Work for her endless patience and guidance in mentoring me through this narrative and my own professional career.

As a graduate student, I had the difficult assignment of working with incarcerated mothers who had their infants with them at a large correctional facility. This story describes my experience with the competing demands which are present within such a system: competition between concern for clients' welfare; and the social worker's responsibility to retain a focus on the governing bureaucracy.

I was outposted in an agency that advocated for incarcerated mothers, but spent most of my time working inside the women's jail. I made this choice because of the conflicts that were present at the small agency in which I was placed. Working in the jail's restrictive environment appeared to me as the better decision.

The "nursery" housed 10 mothers and their infants. I felt glad to get to that part of the facility after passing through several series of barred gates. In the "nursery," painted in baby pastels, the mothers' cells lined up against the walls of a square which formed a middle area for cribs, rocking chairs, TV, other family items, and a children's play area. There was an enclosed outdoor area used by the mothers to wheel their babies around in strollers. The "nursery," as the rest of the prison, was under the constant supervision of uniformed correction officers.

The culture of the prison hierarchy automatically gave special privileges to those inmates "in power." The sameness of guards, and those being guarded was striking, particularly in this facility. The population mirrored the tightly knit neighborhoods from which they had come. Everyone knew everyone else and occasionally it happened that a guard who had been arrested, "became" one of the guarded.

Due to their special circumstance, the incarcerated mothers were separated from most of the other prison population. They were considered uppermost in the prison hierarchy, along with the pregnant women who had yet to deliver. It was always disturbing to visit the hospital locked ward where woman in labor were handcuffed to their bed rails guarded by correction officers.

Individual and group counseling was provided to these women, along with supervision of their parenting skills. Most of these women had other children in some form of placement. I was expected to advocate for their parental rights with foster parents, and extended families where their children had been placed. It was always a systemic challenge.

This program was the ultimate in family preservation treatment, at least for the mothers, and fathers with visiting rights that were incarcerated elsewhere on the grounds. The "nursery" was a time-limited option, much dependent upon the child's birthday and the mothers' sentencing. Children could not stay past their second birthday and if the mother were sentenced to any length of time, she was moved to another prison where such in-house programs did not exist. Critics have argued that the loss and separation experienced by mother and child, coupled with the restricted environment, often outweigh any bonding benefit gained during their time together.

Other women's issues that were relative to these mothers' needs cast constant anxiety on their day to day life. The most evident was their child's second year birthday: the mothers counted the days on their calendars with red and black Xs, as if counting down to the electric chair. Extraordinary preparation and group support surrounded this shared tragedy.

The other overriding theme was the women's experience with sexuality within the prison. Despite that fact that some women became pregnant after being incarcerated, the Corrections Department refused to supply safe sex paraphernalia and sex education because officially "there is (sic) no need, they're not having sex."

There was denial by the Department that there were widespread lesbian relationships; and of the women's concern about HIV/AIDS prevalent among the population. As a student in a large bureaucracy, I had suggested, what appeared to be the impossible to the formal structure: the distribution of condoms, dams, and safe sex education groups. I realized that although the formal structure considered these items contraband, the informal structure had a steady stream of drug contraband flowing into the women's correctional facility. Something was wrong with this picture.

A woman named Tyrae confirmed my feelings about the dilemma. Tyrae was 25 years old, a multi-ethnic woman of color, and the mother of Jamal, her 2 year old son who was with her. Tyrae was on her second incarceration for drug trafficking, and in the prison's methadone program (which was a daily assembly line) for her heroin addiction. Jamal's father also awaited trial in prison for similar charges. The parents had an intact relationship and planned to reunite in their neighborhood after finishing their sentences. Tyrae's 7 year old daughter lived with her parents. Tyrae's father was the police officer that had her investigated and arrested for drug trafficking. He was determined that she would "learn her lesson or die." Despite the unyielding expectations, communication between Tyrae and her family was good, although her father refused to visit her, saying, "I won't see my grandson behind bars, that's no place for a baby." Her mother visited frequently; and used her strong religious beliefs as the framework to encourage Tyrae.

My weekly intervention with Tyrae consisted of supporting her day to day needs while being an advocate and bridge to the free world, and planning for her release. Tyrae was one of the "lucky" ones as she only had 9 months remaining on her sentence. I am hesitant to use the term "lucky" as Tyrae's perspective on the remaining time ranged from the opposite of victimized to ambivalent. For her, day-to-day life was protective as opposed to restrictive, and routine as opposed to chaotic. Things were certain in contrast to uncertain, clean instead of filthy, provided instead of poverty. This is not to paint a glamorous picture of incarceration, but for Tyrae and some others like her, there almost seemed to be a choice—to be incarcerated and "cared for," as opposed to being "free" to be downwardly mobile in the street.

Basic human needs often precipitate the notion "starting where the client is," and can simultaneously present a spark of hope for, at least, a desire for change. The multiproblem, multineed situation presented by Tyrae's impending release was in sharp contrast to matching client to services that were almost nonexistent, and public attitudes which would continue to harden over the next 9 months.

Tyrae possessed several strengths and competencies on which I tried to focus. It seemed that several "systems" had long focused on her mistakes. I sought to redirect this energy. The pending changes that would alter her life space seemed to motivate her to make positive change in her internal focus. Tyrae's motivation was future oriented in that she embraced change, not entirely because of past events, she wanted a different and better future. She desperately wanted to succeed as a mother, lover, and daughter, and knew that the lack of financial and emotional independence were barriers to achieving these goals, once she was released.

Tyrae had sexual relations with another mother in the "nursery." She explained that she was not a lesbian, "It's just to satisfy me in here." She was one of the women concerned with safe sex who had requested contraband dams. I initially responded within the policies of the bureaucracy. I explained that her request was out of the question as it was against the prison rules. However, sometime after the first few months of my field placement in the correctional facility my perspective changed. I was always glad to drive across the bridge from the prison, and on home, but I started to realize why I was glad. I was glad because I hated the smell, I hated the food, I hated the guards, I hated the hierarchy, I hated the attitude, I hated the rules, and most of all, I hated being locked up! My appreciation for my freedom sparked my advocacy toward the women, particularly Tyrae. I was no longer just on the outside looking in. It began when I listened to, and became connected with Tyrae's needs and pain. We started to work as a team to accomplish the end while considering the means. (I might add that as a zealous student, I was caught up in the militant milieu of the environment, but still had enough restraint to survive field placement.)

Although the mothers' needs were provided for in terms of baby things, we could occasionally bring in through the gates a toy, Pampers, and other such things. These items were searched by hand as well as by metal detector wands.

Of course, as I have said, the informal structure really ran the facility. Many of the inmates, including Tyrae, had readily acknowledged the receipt of "contraband" in the form of protection, not only from visitors, but also from the guards themselves.

I explored this further, intrigued by the obvious double standard of the system. Needless to say, it was not difficult to find evidence of this as Tyrae was thrilled to death upon receipt of a package of dams from the outside after she confirmed that her woman partner was HIV positive. If you are wondering about her hiding the dams, much less using the dams, I can assure you that the informal hierarchy was more lenient on the inside than in getting through the gate. There was no question that I had made a conscious choice to look the other way concerning the contraband trafficking, thus condoning and passively participating in the activity. The end seemed to justify the means and I occasionally used my position to allow such contraband exchanges in the counseling rooms.

During this time I had befriended three female guards who were compassionate and motherly toward the infants and their mothers in the "nursery." These women seemed to feel bad about their role as guards and tried to down play it as much as possible. I had cautiously approached the subject of safe sex during lunch with the "nursery" guards. Casually we talked about the difficulty the inmates had, particularly around AIDS and being sexually active. The women shared stories and laughed about "looking the other way" when the inmates engaged in sexual activity.

An air of sympathy surrounded the babies in particular with regard to their being incarcerated as extensions of their mothers. This sympathy was key, as was the sameness among the prisoners and guards which fostered cohesiveness and responsibility for one another, allowing me access to the activity in the underground. With my field placement coming to an end I knew that the right of self-determinism could only continue for Tyrae and the other women with the help of others. Several of the guards exercised power collectively and began to smuggle in the contraband to help their sisters. In reading the signs of the times, the future risk was clear. I left the incarcerated "nursery" with a mix of emotions. I knew that during my short stay, I had made little impact on the formal structure, but perhaps the controversy had managed to mobilize the informal one.

There are some obvious ethical and legal conflicts present in this story. During that time I focused my primary responsibility as a social worker toward my client. In the broader perspective I can "justify" my action as advocacy in the name of making services available to incarcerated women, and prevention of HIV/AIDS.

In retrospect, I have read and reread the NASW Code of Ethics and further explored my own dilemmas. I was faced with a situation where I was bombarded in my emotional responses to being surrounded with sights, sounds, and feelings of women like me, mothers existing in cells, dying of AIDS.

I truly struggled with what to do, while it seemed day after day nothing improved for these women. It was not an easy decision for me to make. I am a person who "follows the rules." I still believe this situation was an exception to the rule for me.

As social workers a priority must be set on our relationships with clients. In this extreme scenario, offering the possibility of hope, where systems denied it, was nothing more than humane. The concepts of social workers adhering to values of the profession are sometimes (this time) in conflict with the social worker's ethical responsibility to an employer and in this case, also a University. I have resolved my actions by reflecting on them as "for the greater good," albeit at risk of jeopardy for myself and others. It is difficult to make decisions against "the rules" for many reasons. However, many rules have been based on prejudicial attitudes; and over time, many persons have made the difficult decision to go against them. The ethical and legal dilemmas about safe sex and incarceration may not be on the level of a major civil rights movement, but for me it was the "Right Thing To Do."[1]

The recent film Fried Green Tomatoes (1991 MCA Universal Pictures) comes to mind as Kathy Bates' character, Evelyn Couch, a woman scorned by the lack of respect for women by individuals and society, fights back. Determined to effect change over herself and others, her freedom cry "Towanda" yields power. I can't help but wonder, if even today the prison underground continues to supply the needs of the women in the "nursery." So for all the women in the "nursery," inmate and guard, "Towanda."

REFERENCES

[1]Lee, Spike (Writer, Producer and Director), Ross, Monty, (Co-Producer). (1989) A 40 Acres and a Mule Filmworks Production. A Spike Lee joint "Do The Right Thing." Universal City Studios, (MCA Home Video, 70 Universal City Plaza, Universal City California 91608).

INDIVIDUAL OBLIGATION AND THE LAW

An Essay on "Do the Right Thing"

By Samuel A. Richmond

Samuel A. Richmond is Professor
of Philosophy, Department of Philosophy,
Cleveland State University, Cleveland, OH.
Dr. Richmond had been the Chair of
the Department of Social Work.

Respect for law arises out of our respect for each other. Laws that foster and protect our humanity are worthy of our respect and win our loyalty and obedience. But even when law fails to win in the court of my conscience I respect it if it wins support from the consciences of other persons. For there are times when I wish them to obey a law my conscience supports even though their conscience may view it as unnecessarily burdensome. Hence, whether this law would be supported by other members of the profession and the community at large is relevant to whether it deserves Houston's obedience The Social Work Profession is perhaps unique in that it advocates for those not well served by the law; and we rely on its members to protect our humanity and personality in the dark place of the law. This essay ~ brief survey of theoretical perspectives on the nature of law and individual obligation suggests that one ought not to take law at face value, but to examine the structure of its actual political, economic and social context.

In "Do the Right Thing," A. Houston reports on her experience as a graduate student in a prison placement working with women inmates in a special unit with their children under age two. Dams for the prevention of sexually transmitted disease among women engaging in same-gender sexual activity in the prison were contraband. Houston reports that the response of prison authorities to legalization was that dams were not needed because sexual activity was not supposed to be taking place.

Houston affirms her "conscious choice to look the other way concerning the contraband trafficking thus condoning and passively participating in the activity." She felt her actions justified because they were for the greater good and served as a model of doing the right thing. Her report raises fundamental questions regarding the nature of legal obligation and its relation to professional ethics and individual conscience. What appeared to her to be right appears to some to be wrong. Where law and individual conscience conflict, does one of them have greater authority? What follows are answers to this question selected from the array of theoretical opinion relevant to this question:

Discussion of this question often begins with the classical statement by Thomas Aquinas of the natural law theory of the relation between legal obligation and moral obligation. According to this view individual conscience is not obligated by law that is contrary to human good:

> either in respect to the ends, as when an authority imposes on his subjects burdensome laws, conducive, not to the common good, but rather to his own cupidity or vainglory; or in respect of the author, as when a man makes a law that goes beyond the power committed to him; or in respect to the form as when burdens are imposed unequally on the community, although with a view to the common good. Such are acts of violence rather than laws, because, as Augustine says, a law that is not just seems to be no law at all. Wherefore such laws do not bind in conscience, except perhaps in order to avoid scandal or disturbance....

For Aquinas, a necessary condition of legal obligation is consistency with moral obligation: law inconsistent with morality cannot obligate; it is no law at all.

A sharply contrasting view is put forth in the classic statement of the positivist theory of the law by the utilitarian, John Austin. For him legal obligation is not a form of moral obligation. It is based on the power of the superior party to coerce obedience. Austin did not assume that the commands of the sovereign were for the common good. Neither did he think they were less obligating when not for the common good. We may be legally obliged to perform acts that are outrageously immoral.

Neither Aquinas nor Austin held that one is morally obliged to obey an unjust law. Nor did they hold that one is morally obligated to disobey. The idea of disobedience motivated by moral obligation was introduced by Henry David Thoreau's refusal to pay his poll tax. According to him, law based on power is corrupt. He claimed individuals are obligated morally to find a way to disobey when law commands and maintains slavery or unjust war. Socrates stands almost alone as one who believes he rightly chose to obey the law even in an instance in which it was clearly unjust. He himself was unjustly sentenced to death and he argued he ought to comply rather than escape, and so he drank the hemlock. But he did not generalize from this instance to argue that one might act unjustly toward another in order to obey a law.

Since World War II, scholarly theories of law include second order rules or principles for the recognition of valid legislation and denial of invalid legislation. No contemporary academic theory of justice would fail to provide for individual disobedience to laws contrary to individual moral opinion, though each might conceive of its proper exercise differently. All believe that one must have a critical view of law; one cannot assume that because something is required by law one ought to comply. Obedience to law just as much as disobedience requires an individual to judge whether what is required is worthy of one's compliance.

It is perhaps the one great lesson of the twentieth century that one ought not comply with laws that require one to treat others in ways that conflict with one's conscience. According to Gandhi and King we are morally obliged where necessary to join together in organized collective disobedience to remove unjust laws. A policy of continued compliance is not morally permissible in their view.

Continental traditions of philosophical reflection on the law tend to be more critical than Anglo-American. Karl Marx viewed law in a capitalist system as inevitably in the interest of the ruling class and contrary to the interests of the working class; according to Vladimir Lenin, the State is armed men and prisons in the service of the capitalist class and at war against the working class. Sigmund Freud saw civilization as the source of internal conflicts that pit individuals against themselves.

Jean-Paul Sartre and Michel Foucault hold that there is no politically neutral moral resolution to the conflicts of contemporary humanity, but that we are constantly faced with the problem of doing the right thing in an environment of power that corrupts our thought and discourse. Jacques Derrida in a critique of Walter Benjamin in "The Force of Law" contends that there is no justification of the violence of the law—none. .

Historically, the force of law has been exercised in wars of national aggression, slavery, systematic oppression of women and persons of subpopulations differing in religion, caste, language, nationality, or other condition of birth. It is only in recent years that law has been an instrument for ending slavery, protecting rights, and extending freedom.

Robin West and Margaret Jane Radin, feminist critics of American law, have noted its history. Laws that govern women have paternalistic roots. Women's perspectives are not routinely represented in the law. There has been no systematic purge from law of this long-accumulated bias against women. The Equal Rights Amendment is designed to eliminate inequalities based on gender from the legal system. Women do not yet have constitutional protection from unjust legislation.

The brief survey of theoretical perspectives on the nature of law and individual obligation does not give much support to the view that there is a prima facie moral obligation to obey the law simply because it is the law. To the contrary, each school of thought alerts us to sources of criticism of the law which may invalidate its claim to individual obedience. What are the sources and aim of the law? What function does it actually serve? Who does it actually serve? Are those governed by it among its authors?

Theoretical reflection on law suggests one ought not to take law at face value but to examine the structure of its actual political, economic, and social context. Does the law serve the common good? Does it burden people equitably and in proportion to their means regardless of differences of race, gender, religion, language, nationality, economic class, or social position, or other condition of birth? Is it within the authority of its author? Does it impose slavery or war on others? Does it serve the interests of one economic class at costs to interests of another? Does it divide human personality against itself or enhance its integrity? Does it rely on a pious lie, ideology, or power discourse whereby the conditions of its application are taken to be as they are supposed to be rather than as they are actually? Is the law itself a significant source of violence in the population? Law that commands obedience morally must meet high moral expectations.

When we ask these questions of the law denying dams to women in a jail in which sexual activity is taking place among inmates some of whom have tested HIV positive, many potential sources of invalidity appear. Few would allow that it is for the common good, since it risks increase in the incidence among inmates and in the general population. What ends does denying dams serve? Is such an end a proper aim of legislation? Is denying dams a proper means given the risks?

Does denying women in prison dams distribute the burdens of pursuit of the aims of the laws equitably? Placing women in prison at greater risk for incurring sexually transmitted disease places a disproportional burden of risk upon them. Drug laws of recent years have placed the burden unequally on lower-income classes. Disproportionate mandated sentencing accounts for most of the increased imprisonment of low-income people.

In recent years the larger context of law in which prison laws function has become an instrument for shifting burdens from those of great means to those of small means. Income and wealth have been redistributed from the bottom up. The impoverishment of the low-income people has had disastrous effects. Higher rates of imprisonment is one. Higher prison rates are an especially burdensome imposition on the least advantaged of our society.

What the law is depends upon actual practices of the law and the view of those practices held by conscientious citizens. Where the informal or actual practice is consistently and predictably different from the text of the law, the practice of the law may be a better guide to what the law actually is. Legal interpretation includes reference to practice, it takes into account limits in effectiveness, and it relies on the judgment of reasonable persons to interpret its meaning and decide its validity. The expectations of reasonable persons administering the law and governed by the law are in turn shaped as much by practice as text.

Deference to individual conscience is built into law. The law is decided by judge and jury, and will they not assume the validity of their conscientious reflection in making decisions of law? Would we want them to act otherwise? Only those acts that survive the test of conscience rightly receive the sanctions of law.

Is looking the other way or more actively facilitating transfer of the means of disease prevention a form of fraud, deceit or misrepresentation that is inconsistent with the values of members of the profession of social workers or the larger community? What is the view of the faculties of schools of social work on whether denial of the dams is just? What is the view of the members of the National Association of Social Workers whose Code of Ethics is to guide us here? Prison systems involve us in contradictions that reach to our deepest values and sentiments. We rely on persons of good conscience to act with due consideration and discerning judgment that assigns high priority to the actual advancement of human life, human health, and human personality.

Covertly facilitating the transfers of dams does not seem to be an act that shows any disrespect for anyone. The prison system and the community at large are not as such persons. A fair number of persons within the prison system and the community at large seem to agree with Houston's assessment of the justness of the denial of dams to women in prison. She sought to entrench the availability of this source of protection by directly participating in the prison's informal structure of support.

Note that it may be illegal to possess or transfer other forms of prison contraband such as drugs and guns outside of prison settings. Possession and transfer of dams is not inherently illegal; it is illegal only in prison. Note, too, that participating in the covert transfer of dams is not like vigilante justice in which violence is used against others who have been judged to act contrary to the wishes of the vigilantes.

Respect for law arises out of our respect for each other. Laws that foster and protect our humanity are worthy of our respect and win our loyalty and obedience. But even when law fails to win in the court of my conscience I respect it if it wins support from the consciences of other persons. For there are times when I wish them to obey a law my conscience supports even though their conscience may view it as unnecessarily burdensome. Hence, whether this law would be supported by other members of the profession and the community at large is relevant to whether it deserves Houston's obedience.

Discussions of civil disobedience often note that disobedience should be done publicly and with a willingness to accept the consequences—the punishments prescribed by the law for those who violate it. Where disobedience may appear to serve both one's conscience and one's personal interests, as in conscientious refusal to perform military service, one might accept punishment, or an alternative risk of one's own life in the service of others, in order to demonstrate good faith. And where the goal is freedom and equality for an oppressed people, a willingness to suffer some of the consequences of disobedience in order to eliminate unjust laws may be necessary to keep the focus of other citizens on change. But there is no inherent reason for those who disobey unjust laws to suffer punishment. Suffering such sanctions arises from the need to show respect to citizens with whom one disagrees but whom one hopes to persuade by earnest action. It was unjust that Martin Luther King was locked in the Birmingham jail because the law which placed him there was unjust law.

Would we want no one under a Hitlerist or Stalinist regime to disobey to protect another person without doing so publicly and with acceptance of punishment? Would we want those who did so punished later? Houston reports seeking to change the prison practice publicly but unsuccessfully. Covert disobedience incurs additional risks that moral agents must take into account. It alienates and isolates people from each other.

Conflicts between individuals and the law often have to do with the tension between the hypothetical conditionals that are supposed to be the case under the law and what is actually the case. Thus the argument that there need be no protection because there is not supposed to be any sexual activity. Sometimes the human heart responds with compassion to what is actually the case and views as merely theoretical that which is supposed to be but is not. Moreover, it is difficult for the law to guide us under conditions that are contrary-to-law. Recognition and public discussion are often proscribed as well. Few wish to be perceived as urging violation of law for that itself may be proscribed. As a result the dictates of man-made law benefit from subordination to the dictates of the individual human heart. Would we have it otherwise? Would we have every decision so legalistic as to be premised only on how things are supposed to be without regard to how they actually are?

Social work students sometimes bring a fresh perspective to corrections settings. For example, a student in a sentencing setting lobbied for prisoners being told that no mail from home would be forwarded to them the first month of incarceration rather than believe no one had written. The court changed its practice. Had the court not changed, would we want no social worker or student to tell any inmate the true reason they were not receiving any mail? We hope all will subject their actions to a close examination of their relationship to the ethical codes of our professions and individual conscience. A profession that depends on law for its recognition and license is bound to fidelity to what is sound in the law. Social work is perhaps unique in that it advocates for those not served well by the law. And we rely on the members of this profession to protect our humanity and personality in the dark place of the law.

ADVOCACY OR UNETHICAL PRACTICE

On "Do The Right Thing"

3b

By Sheldon R. Gelman

Sheldon R. Gelman Ph.D., ACSW,
MSL is Dorothy and David I.
Schachne Dean, Wurzweiler
School of Social Work,
Yeshiva University, NY, NY.

Social workers' behavior and actions are guided by a Code of Ethics. We are not lone rangers or vigilantes on a crusade to right the perceived wrongs inflicted by impersonal bureaucracies. We are employed in host settings and are taught how to bring about change in individuals, groups, organizations and communities. We place ourselves, our clients, and our profession at risk when we violate rules and regulations, and undermine authority.

My reaction to the article, "Do the Right Thing" by Annie L. Houston, as a reviewer was so intense that in addition to writing my review I expressed my concerns to the editor. The decision of the Executive Board of Reflections to publish it with responses by educators should serve as both a teaching exercise and as a means of stimulating critical practice analysis.

43

Social workers are professionals whose behavior and actions are guided by a Code of Ethics. We are not lone rangers or vigilantes on a crusade to right the perceived wrongs inflicted by impersonal bureaucracies. We are employed in host settings and are taught how to bring about change in individuals, groups, organizations and communities. We place ourselves, our clients, and our profession at risk when we violate rules and regulations, and undermine authority.

Being a change agent and advocate involves both responsibilities and consequences. Advocacy is a means to an end, not an end in itself. To be a successful advocate, one must understand both the role and the environment in which one functions. While the client's wants and needs are critical to the process, not all clients' needs are legitimate nor are they necessarily appropriate or attainable. Respect for the worth and dignity of clients extends to our colleagues and employers as well as our clients.

In addition to the concerns stated above, I felt that the author, by submitting for publication a paper in which she chronicled her behaviors, was ethically vulnerable herself, and jeopardized both her university and their ability to utilize this facility as a field placement site in the future. It was also troubling to me that she appeared to function without supervision and that her faculty advisor had not raised these issues with her.

It has long been recognized that the criminal justice system is faced with the often conflicting objectives of protecting society and rehabilitating the offender. The author would have been well served to have reviewed the goals and objectives relating to correctional policy before writing off the system and identifying so strongly with her client's wants and circumstances. Given my background in corrections, this particular program and setting appears to have provided an enlightened, if not innovative, approach to dealing with convicted female offenders who are pregnant and/ or have very young children. The setting provided opportunities in which appropriate interventions could have brought about positive change in clients as well as broader systemic innovation.

The practice of social work in such settings is difficult at best, and requires a delicate balancing of roles. It is unfortunate that the student appeared to dismiss the learning opportunities and resources of program and facility staff. Her actions mirrored those of the one not engaged in professional education. The system's failure to act appropriately in enforcing policies does not provide license for a social work professional to engage in rule violation.

While the Code of Ethics teaches us that our primary responsibility is to our clients and that the worker is to make every effort to foster maximum self-determination on the part of clients, the Code also requires the worker to treat colleagues with respect, courtesy, and fairness, and to adhere to commitments made to the employing organization.

In this particular situation it could be argued that the worker had obligations to multiple systems which includes the prison system, the community at large, as well as clients. Pursuing the interests of one set of clients over the interests of others without fully comprehending the competing interests is incorrect.

Social workers should maintain high standards of personal conduct, should act in accordance with the highest standard of professional integrity and should not participate in, condone, or be associated with dishonesty, fraud, deceit, or misrepresentation. Violation of these ethical principles are grounds for dismissal in every social work education program in the nation.

The author's misguided belief that somehow she was righting a wrong or assisting her clients in becoming self-determining or independent is inadequate justification for engaging in unprofessional and potentially dangerous behavior. This is not, unfortunately, a women's issue, or an issue of power, it is an issue of proper practice and ethical behavior. Unfortunately, even after reflecting on the ethical issues involved, the author fails to identify with the principles of the Code of Ethics in assessing her practice. To write about practice without understanding the core issues involved is both frightening and sad.

COMMENT ON "DO THE RIGHT THING"

3c

By Mary Ann Jimenez

Mary Ann Jimenez, Ph.D. is
Professor, The Department of
Social Work, California State
University Long Beach,
Long Beach, CA.

The author demonstrated her commitment to the profession of social work even as she ignored the rules of the institution in which she was placed. When human life and well being are at stake, as in the case of prison inmates who did not have the means to protect themselves from HIV infection during sexual contact, then a social worker is justified in rule breaking. Is this not at the heart of our profession, whose commitment to social justice, human dignity and client empowerment has distinguished it from all other professions since its inception?

When prison officials implicitly allowed sexual contact to occur between inmates, inmates should have the power to protect themselves from life-threatening disease. Social workers are not only employees or students placed in custodial institutions. Like other professionals, we have a broader commitment—to the ethics of our profession and to our own consciences. Social workers who have been activists in social and political struggles in the past have been forced to break institutional rules (the rules about needle exchange for drug users come to mind). This story was no exception to this tradition.

ON DOING THE RIGHT THING

By Frederic G. Reamer, Ph.

Frederic G. Reamer, Ph.D., is
Professor, School of Social Work, Rhode Island College, Providence RI.
He serves as chair of the NASW (National Association of Social Work)
Code of Ethics Revision Committee and the NASW—Rhode Island Committee
on Inquiry. He is also a member of the State of Rhode Island Parole Board.

Our aim is to figure out which duty or obligation should take precedence over the others, assuming that one of them must rise to the top of the entangled heap. I argue in this brief commentary that ethical decision-making needs to include a number of components if it is to be meaningful. Ethical decision-making is a difficult, sometimes agonizingly prolonged process, not merely an event and involves a series of problem-solving steps.

A number of years ago, I worked in a maximum security penitentiary. One of my responsibilities was to facilitate a treatment group for inmates. All of the inmates in this group (usually about 10) were serving lengthy sentences for crimes such as murder, aggravated assault, rape, robbery, arson, and drug selling.

One afternoon, after our group's meeting had ended, I was walking through the prison yard when one of the group's members approached me. This was a fellow who was serving a 25-year sentence for second-degree murder. I would say that this inmate and I had a very good working relationship. He respected me and my role, I think, and I was able to behave respectfully toward him (the fact that this man had matured tremendously in prison certainly helped me to respect him). As I walked through the prison yard with this inmate, he furtively slipped an envelope in my hand and asked me to keep walking. I was a bit startled, of course. The inmate then told me that he needed to mail a letter to his dying brother and asked that I drop the envelope in a mailbox outside the prison's walls. The inmate commented that the prison policy prohibiting him from mailing such a letter, because it was addressed to a former inmate, was unjust. I could understand the inmate's frustration (assuming what he told me was true), although I also understood why prison administrators wanted to prevent communication between inmates and former inmates. Clearly, the inmate was asking me to smuggle contraband outside the prison walls (which, by the way, is the direction opposite that in which contraband usually travels).

Given the circumstances, the timing, and the setting, I wasn't able to pause and ponder the situation at the moment. So as not to cause a scene and, frankly, to wiggle my way out of this awkward and immediate predicament, I simply nodded my head, slipped the envelope into my pants pocket, and kept on walking. Between the time of the incident and my departure for the day, I had forgotten about the letter. As I left the prison, I instinctively reached into my pants pocket to see what was taking up all that room and realized at that point that I had inadvertently walked out of the prison with contraband. "Now what do I do?" I thought. For a moment I considered dropping the letter in a mailbox, but ultimately decided not to. Three things occurred to me. First, what message would I be conveying to this inmate if I went along with his illegal scheme? Wouldn't I be reinforcing his "criminal ways" and, at least indirectly, condoning the kind of behavior that landed him in prison in the first place? Second, wouldn't it be unethical to knowingly violate the prison policy that prohibits mailed communications of this sort? Was the policy so unjust that such "civil disobedience" was warranted? Finally, might I not get in some kind of trouble—perhaps even big trouble—if it became known that I smuggled the contraband outside the prison? Who would believe my defense that I had completely forgotten that the envelope was in my pocket, only to discover it after I had walked through the last prison gate? Was it really worth the risk?

My memory of this incident flashed back to me as I read Annie Houston's account. Houston describes what all seasoned social workers have encountered at some point during their careers: circumstances that require a difficult ethical choice (some more difficult than others, to be sure). Houston's predicament is certainly unique in a number of ways—the unique constellation of individuals' personalities and idiosyncrasies, institutional features, organizational politics, racial and ethnic issues, and interpersonal intrigue—but it also shares some common traits. Houston's scenario contains an ethical dilemma's two key ingredients: (1) the emergence of specific professional duties and obligations. (in this scenario, empowering clients, respecting clients' rights to self-determination and confidentiality, complying with agency policy); and (2) some sort of clash between these various professional duties and obligations (Houston's wish to empower her clients and respect their right to self-determination and confidentiality collided with her presumed duty to comply with agency policy concerning inmate access to contraband and participation in prohibited activities).

To use the language of ethics, Houston's ethical dilemma, and for that matter every ethical dilemma, involves difficult choices between and among what the philosopher W. D. Ross calls prima facie obligations and duties (prima facie duties and obligations are those we are inclined to fulfill ceteris paribus, all things being equal). Our aim is to figure out which duty or obligation should take precedence over the others, assuming that one of them must rise to the top of the entangled heap (what Ross calls one's actual duty).

Fortunately, contemporary social workers, unlike their predecessors, have access to a wide range of conceptual tools to help them navigate ethical storms that appear during their careers, whether they pertain to work with individuals, families, couples, and groups (for example, conflicts between a client's right to confidentiality and a social worker's obligation to disclose confidential information to protect a third party from imminent harm, or between a vulnerable client's right to self-determination and the social worker's duty to protect the client from engaging in self-destructive activity); nonclinical issues such as how one ought to allocate scarce resources (what are called issues of distributive justice) or, as in this case, whether one must always obey a law or an agency regulation; or relationships among professional colleagues (for example, how to handle situations where a colleague has behaved unethically). Especially since the early 1980s, social workers and members of other helping professions have produced a rich collection of writings on ethical dilemmas, the application of ethical theory, and ethical decision-making.

My principal claim here is that there is, indeed, a way to think systematically about ethical dilemmas of the sort faced by Houston. Ethical dilemmas warrant rigorous exploration in much the same way that clinical, community organizing, advocacy, and administrative dilemmas in practice warrant rigorous exploration. What seasoned social worker would be willing to tackle such complicated tasks without some systematic education about, study of, and deliberation concerning all important facets of the situation? It's unthinkable. I believe that ethical dilemmas deserve the same sort of attention.

I certainly understand Houston's wish to be helpful to the inmates with whom she worked. That's normal, especially in an oppressive prison, although social workers would likely disagree among themselves about whether "looking the other way" as the women received contraband and engaged in prohibited activities was the wisest way to react. And it's admirable that Houston consulted the NASW Code of Ethics to see whether the document contained any useful guidance.

But I would argue that ethical decision-making needs to include a number of other components if it is to be meaningful. Ethical decision-making is a difficult, sometimes agonizingly prolonged process, not merely an event. Ethical decision-making involves a series of problem-solving steps, as do all other domains of social work practice.

Here are the steps I would take were I in Houston's shoes (this is a necessarily superficial overview; see Reamer, 1995, for a more complete discussion of this approach):

1. Identify the ethical issues, including the social work values and duties that conflict. As I mentioned above, the principal conflict in this case is between the social worker's obligation to empower clients and respect clients' rights to self-determination and confidentiality, on the one hand, and, on the other hand, the obligation to comply with agency policy.

2. Identify the individuals, groups, and organizations who are likely to be affected by the ethical decision. Those most likely to be affected in this case are the inmates, prison administrators, the social worker herself, and the university. Inmates stand to gain if the social

worker "looks the other way" when they receive contraband and engage in prohibited activities; they stand to lose if the social worker enforces prison regulations. (I suppose one could also argue that inmates ultimately would lose if their social worker implicitly or explicitly condones, and thereby reinforces, activity that violates rules or laws.) Prison administrators stand to gain if the social worker enforces its regulations (unless one argues that inmates who are denied their contraband and sexual activity will stir up trouble for the administrators); they stand to lose if the social worker or other staff deliberately undermine their authority and regulations. The social worker stands to gain if she believes that her primary obligation is to empower inmates; she stands to lose if she knowingly violates prison regulations, exposes herself to institutional discipline, and jeopardizes her own job (or, in this case, field placement) and career. The university stands to gain if Houston's actions do not lead to a strain in its relationship with the prison; the university stands to lose if prison officials discover Houston's deliberate violation of regulations and, consequently, are critical of the university's teaching or supervision.

3. Tentatively identify all possible courses of action and the participants involved in each, along with the possible risks and benefits. Houston's overview of her dilemma suggests that there was a fairly stark choice between complying with the prison's regulations and "looking the other way." I wonder, however, whether there might be some middle ground. I would like to know, for example, whether Houston approached prison administrators to discuss her concerns or advocated for some sort of policy that would protect inmates who engaged in sexual contact. Having worked in prisons, I know how recalcitrant prison officials can be. But I've also been surprised on occasion with the effectiveness of assertive, yet diplomatic advocacy efforts. One of the greatest lessons I've learned over the years about ethical dilemmas is that the choice rarely involves a simple "either-or." Very often, there are many shades of gray between the white and black options. Skillful social workers can use their talent and acumen to identify options others may not have considered and facilitate meaningful discussion of them, manage conflict that emerges, and move participants in the direction of a reasonable resolution.

4. Thoroughly examine the reasons in favor of and opposed to each possible course of action, considering relevant ethical theories, principles, and guidelines; codes of ethics and legal principles; social

work practice theory and principles; and personal values. It's not clear to me to what extent Houston attempted to track down social work literature on ethical decision-making and ethical theory, for example. This case provides a prototypical example of the ways in which classical ethical theory might help one think through how a difficult case ought to be handled. The so-called deontological perspective in moral theory, for instance, suggests that people have a fundamental obligation to obey laws, regulations, and so forth. In this case, deontology, a perspective embraced by Immanuel Kant, would likely suggest that Houston's principal obligation was to obey and enforce prison policy. In contrast, the so-called teleological or consequentialist perspective, typically associated with John Stuart Mill and Jeremy Bentham, suggests that one's ethical duty is determined by the nature of the consequences. An act utilitarian, for example, would argue that Houston should have weighed all of the likely "pluses" and "minuses" associated with the possible courses of action and pursue the course of action that is likely to yield the greatest balance of pluses over minuses (the greatest net "gain"). A rule utilitarian, however, would argue that it would be short-sighted to engage in this sort of calculus only as it pertains to this immediate case. From this point of view, the lens needs to be broadened to include the potential long-term consequences resulting from reinforcing inmates' deception and rule violation, providing inmates with a role model who condones deception and rule violation, and undermining institutional policy. Thus, from a rule utilitarian perspective, perhaps the social worker should not have violated the prison rules, whereas an act utilitarian perspective might have been used to justify breaking prison rules to empower the inmates.

Unfortunately, space does not permit full exploration of the relevance of these and other ethical theories, the NASW Code of Ethics, or social work practice theory and principles. Suffice it to say that these sources should be carefully considered because of their potential to help practitioners thoroughly examine the diverse ethical issues facing them.

5. Consult with colleagues and appropriate experts. Here too it's not clear to what extent Houston consulted with other prison staff, supervisors, attorneys, or ethics experts. Generally speaking, social workers should take time to locate thoughtful colleagues who may be able to offer valuable insight and opinions. Consultants won't necessarily provide unequivocal advice, but they may help to sort out various

arguments and counter arguments, and they may help identify significant blind spots.

Certainly there is lots of room for legitimate debate about whether social workers should always obey the law, agency policies, and regulations. Although a strict deontological perspective suggests that laws, policies, and regulations should always be obeyed, most social workers can think of extreme instances when it may be justifiable, on ethical grounds, to violate them. There is no doubt in my mind that there is a place for principled civil disobedience, in the spirit of such luminaries as Henry David Thoreau, Martin Luther King, Jr., and Mahatma Gandhi (Childress, 1971).

In general, however, I think it's a mistake for social workers to take matters into their own hands and violate laws, policies, and regulations when it merely seems expedient or convenient to do so. In my mind, deliberate violation of laws, policies, and regulations demands extraordinary circumstances—for example, where lives are at stake or clients' most basic needs are threatened—and remarkably compelling evidence that no reasonable alternative exists. As Campbell (1991: 178) notes, "the functional and symbolic purposes of law in our society entail that its violation by acts of civil disobedience should be a last resort. That is, all other reasonable alternatives to redress wrongs and grievances ... should be exhausted before resort to civil disobedience is advocated." Moreover, social workers who decide to violate laws, policies, and regulations must be willing to challenge that which they deem to be unjust and be willing to accept whatever penalties or sanctions might come their way.

Whether Houston's circumstances and actions meet this test is not for me to decide alone, particularly since I know only what I read about them and was not directly involved in the situation. I must confess, however, that this sort of insurgent social work makes me nervous, because of its potential to undermine organizational stability and convey the wrong moral message to clients. Houston concedes that she "made a conscious choice to look the other way concerning the contraband trafficking, thus condoning and passively participating in the activity. The end seemed to justify the means and I occasionally used my position and presence to allow such contraband exchanges privately in counseling rooms." However, as Campbell (1991: 174) astutely asserts with respect to the complicated argument that the ends justify the means, "the fundamental, though not sufficient, criterion for the justification of civil disobedience is to justify the cause.... The ends do have to justify the means, but this does not entail that the ends themselves are immune from moral scrutiny." I would like to hear more about Houston's claim that the ends (permitting inmates to engage in prohibited activity and have access to contraband) are sufficiently compelling to justify the means (the deliberate violation of prison regulations).

This sort of ethical dilemma is hardly new, as illustrated by Sophocles' play Antigone. Antigone, the daughter of Oedipus, wanted to bury her brother, Polynice, who had been killed by their brother Eteocles. Creon, the king of Thebes, forbade the burial, however, because Polynice was a rebel. Antigone challenged what she believed was the king's unjust order by giving her brother a proper burial:

Creon: "Now tell me, in as few words as you can, did you know the order forbidding such an act?"

Antigone: "I knew it, naturally. It was plain enough."

Creon: "And yet you dared to contravene it"?

Antigone: "Yes. That order did not come from God. Justice, that dwells with the gods below, knows no such law. I did not think your edicts strong enough to overrule the unwritten unalterable laws of God and heaven, you being only a man."

REFERENCES

Campbell, Courtney S. (1991). Ethics and militant AIDS activism. In F. G. Reamer (Ed.), AIDS and ethics (pp. 155–187). New York: Columbia University Press.

Childress, James F. (1971). Civil disobedience and political obligation. New Haven: Yale University Press.

Reamer, Frederic G. (1995). Social work values and ethics. New York: Columbia University Press.

BETWEEN THE AGENCY
AND THE UNIVERSITY

By Janet Black

Janet Black is Director of
Field Education, Department of
Social Work, California State
University, Long Beach, CA.

*An interdependent relationship must exist
between the university and the agency in providing field education. The behaviors and interactions of each partner are inexplicably related;
one individual's disregard for the partnership
may result in unsuccessful learning experiences
and disruption of service and education.*

As I read the narrative recounting Ms Houston's
experience as a student in a corrections field
work placement, along with the strategy she
chose to deal with her concerns, I became more
and more uncomfortable and concerned. By the
end of the article, I was distressed and alarmed
about what had occurred. Questions began coming forward faster than I could write them
down: Where was the field instructor (agency
staff) during this period? Was adequate supervision being provided to the student? Where was

57

the university faculty field liaison (employed by the university as liaison between the agency and the university) during this period? Was adequate consultation and support being provided to both the student and the agency field instructor? What might be the consequences of the student's actions on the agency, on the individual field instructor, on the university, on the student, on the director of field education? Can the previously crafted university/ agency agreement withstand the potential negative consequences of such an experience?

As a Director of Field Education at a large, public university, placing approximately 600 BASW and MSW students each year, I am intimately aware of the interdependent relationship that must exist between the university and its participating field work agencies. The behaviors and interactions of each partner are inexplicably related to each other; any one individual's disregard for the whole partnership system will result in unsatisfying and unsuccessful teaching and learning experiences, or worse, in disruption of partnerships that were developed to provide service and education to both parties.

I can't help but wonder if the field instructor was aware of the student's observations and concerns, or aware of the potential consequences of the actions Ms Houston took. What guidance might have been provided to enable a planful intervention that included all levels of the agency system. The field instructor's role as a supervisor and teacher requires assisting students with dilemmas such as this one, and maintaining communication with the student and university partners. The university field department's responsibility to provide consultation and support to both student and field instructor is most critical. I am concerned that these opportunities were overlooked or ignored by all partners.

I believe that our role in field education is to educate both our students and our agency field instructors to a range of intervention strategies, and be "open to learning new systems" ourselves, to become aware of current needs and issues, and incorporate that knowledge in our teaching and curriculum materials.

Avenues for new learning for field directors present themselves in this chapter. When placing students in the corrections system, what issues should we anticipate will confront the student early in their experience; how can we help the student prepare to meet these issues with thoughtful inquiry and responsive interventions that reflect an understanding of the systems perspective and professional responsibilities?

An important step in negotiating an affiliation agreement with a potential field agency is my (Director of Field Education) visit to the agency, to talk with the agency executive and prospective field instructor, and to identify the potential learning experiences, and the potential difficulties or challenges that each setting poses. This allows for mutual expectations and needs to be clearly stated; and an agreement to work together that is consciously designed to achieve the goals and objectives we have set out.

How might a university field liaison have been involved in this student's situation? My experience (and my expectation) has been that field liaisons pay careful attention to concerns about agency policy and service delivery issues raised by students. How exciting to have the opportunity to provide a framework for looking at these issues with the students, and assist them in learning the skills of assessing and planning an intervention to respond to the issues, perhaps gaining a new perspective or vantage point ourselves.

A final series of questions. How might this agency and the university revisit their agreement to work together for future educational activities? What can they learn from this experience to enable both partners to be more conscious of potential issue areas, to jointly prepare students for the experience, to prepare the agency for the experience of having students (some of whom will have strong conflicts with the system's perspective of service delivery), and to assure that communication channels are open and available. How can universities and agencies extend their mutual participation in social work education and service delivery to identify system delivery policies that must become a part of the educational experience?

I am hopeful that these issues, critical to the field work curriculum, continue to be addressed to provide students with a challenging learning experience with educational integrity, and to provide clients with the most appropriate interventions and services.

LETTERS TO
THE EDITOR

Responses to "Do The Right Thing" and accompanying commentaries. *Reflections: Narratives of Professional Helping.* Vol. 2, # 3, Summer 1996

Dear Editor.

I have just finished reading "Do the Right Thing" and the invited commentaries on this narrative in the Summer issue *Reflections*. I believe that Ms. Houston did the right thing, and am surprised by the controversy which has surrounded its publication. I come to this decision based on a series of questions which I posed to myself and the answers I arrived at.

Q: Was there sex going on in the prison when Ms. Houston arrived for her field placement?

A: Yes, and the fact that this rule was broken was the precondition which set up Ms. Houston's dilemma. Had this rule not been broken, there would have been no need for Ms. Houston to take any action regarding the provision of contraband items.

Q: Did Ms. Houston in any way encourage sexual behavior in this setting?

A: No, unless one believes that providing protective devices further encourages sexual behavior, which I do not believe to be the case. Sexual behavior was occurring, and would continue to occur, prior to the provision of dams.

Q: Should Ms. Houston have attempted to stop the sexual behavior which was going on, either formally or informally?

A: While one might argue that this might have been a way for Ms. Houston to have avoided her ethical dilemma, and thus to avoid needing "to engage in rule violation," it would have seriously harmed, if not destroyed, her ability to form relationships with both inmates and staff who were "looking the other way." Without this trust, she could not be an effective social worker within this agency environment. As she states "the informal structure really ran the facility."

Q: Did Ms. Houston break the law by providing the dams and therefore commit a clear violation of her professional ethics?

A: As Samuel Richmond notes: "Possession and transfer of dams is not inherently illegal; it is illegal only in prison." And it is illegal, not due to any "law," but due to an administrative regulation which many social workers would find unacceptable. Is there anyone who has practiced social work who has not broken a bureaucratic regulation when they thought it was in the best interest of our client?

Q: Given that sexual activities were occurring, did Ms. Houston have an ethical obligation to stop the spread of HIV/AIDS?

A: Yes. HIV infection usually leads to death within a decade. And despite recent advances in the medical treatment of HIV infection, marginalized populations are the least able to access either medications to treat the disease or social services to ameliorate its psychosocial impact.

Q: Did provision of barrier dams in any way undermine the goals of the social service program in which Ms. Houston was placed as a student?

A: No. Provision of these "contraband" devices, which were neither destructive or harmful to her clients, helped her gain her client's trust without undermining the programs' purposes. If this program was the "ultimate in family preservation treatment," and Ms. Houston was expected to "advocate for the [prisoners] with foster parents and extended families where their children had been placed" then provision of the dams only furthered the purposes of the program. There can be no family preservation if a mother is incapacitated from or dies of AIDS; there can be no "bonding benefit" at all if the person to whom the infant bonds is dead.

Q: Could the provision of barrier dams further the treatment goals with the client?

A: If one believes in strengths-based treatment then the answer to this question is yes. If Tyrae (the client) was, in fact, "future oriented," and she "wanted to succeed as a mother, lover and daughter," she could only do so if she was healthy and alive. Her concern with safe sex, which led her to approach Ms. Houston about the dams, demonstrates this future orientation, and the provision of the dams may have reinforced this orientation. It certainly reinforced the importance of responsibility in sexual conduct to Tyrae. I believe, in Richmond's words, that the provision of the barrier dams led to the advancement of "human life, human health, and human personality."

Q: Does the "system's failure to act appropriately in enforcing policies... provide license for a social work professional to engage in rule violation?"

A: On this point, I disagree strongly with Gelman's remarks. If the system had enforced its rules about sexual conduct, then the student would not have faced the ethical dilemma she did. However, since the system was not enforcing a rule which led to the ethical dilemma, the student had the obligation to act in the best interest of her client—in this case a life or death interest. I believe that Jiminez is correct when she notes, "when prison officials implicitly allowed sexual contact to occur between inmates, inmates should have the power to protect themselves from life-threatening diseases." In opposition to Reamer, I believe that civil disobedience was warranted in this case, since, in my opinion, the student had "no reasonable alternative" which could have been implemented in a timely manner.

Q: Should Ms. Houston have consulted with appropriate school personnel before pursuing her course of action given the institutional consequences which her actions might have had?

A: There is no question that this should have been the course of action that the student should have pursued. And, we do not know if she did— the narrative, for whatever reason, is silent on this point. One can assume, however, that the student might have pursued such a course since she acknowledges a professor for "guiding (her] through this narrative and (her] own professional career." But even if she had not, or had she been told not to pursue the course of action she did based on institutional considerations, I believe that on ethical grounds the student's actions would have been upheld by a reasonable faculty or field instruction staff.

HIV infection and AIDS are preventable. It is a social worker's obligation to preserve the public health, alleviate potential suffering, and foster the human potential in all of our clients, even if we are hindered by the actions of our government and its agencies. Some, particularly those who have instituted needle exchange programs, have been particularly courageous and broken the law in pursuit of these principles. Others, like Ms. Houston, have broken agency regulations. Still others in our profession work tirelessly to combat the spread of this disease and work compassionately and professionally to tend those afflicted with it. To criticize such efforts as unethical, even if bureaucratic rules are broken or institutional relationships are jeopardized, is to give comfort and ammunition to those who believe that this disease is the just dessert of IV drug users, the poor, people of color, and gay men in our society.

William Meezan
*(The author was formally at the University of
Southern California School of Social Work
and is now at the University of Michigan)*

Reflections,

I am an incarcerated Mother. I have no way to contact Annie Houston through your magazine. I speak for many of my sisters behind bars with me who have heard her article. I am asking please print my words so that Annie and others will know the truth.

Dear Annie.

I am an incarcerated Afro-American mother of three. Last week my caseworker brought me your magazine article "Do The Right Thing." I have shared this with most of my sisters in my block and talked with them about it. Words cannot begin to say the tears of hope and pain that ran down our cheeks as I read your story out loud to those who cannot read. The pain of your description that for us is a day to day existence for we could all be Tyrae. The hope that there are people like you who don't just care but care enough to risk. Hope that people like you can be our connection to another world that treats us as human beings. You brought dignity to women who love each other and want to live. We are humbled by your courage and strength and you must know that you are our hero.

Thank you
Name withheld
Prisoner #16774922

Dear Editor:

This is just a quick note to let you know that I thought the summer issue of *Reflections* was terrific. There is no journal that I know of in social work or other fields that seems as close to real life practice as *Reflections*. The article and response to "Do the Right Thing" were I thought excellent—and raised many thoughtful questions and ethical issues/dilemmas to ponder. I also loved your editorial—the insurrection of subjugated knowledge—was very powerful in directing readers not simply to the content of the articles, but to the manner in which the stories are told. There seem to me to be many layers of embedded narratives implied in Annie Houston's article, such as the guards "looking the other way," which she also emulated—and (in a very interesting parallel) perhaps so did her field instructor, faculty liaison, University etc. Given so much looking away and secret keeping—it is amazing that there was still a stranger's need to tell the story in the form of a narrative. I wonder if Houston has any desire to respond to the comments and criticisms.

J. L. Kayser
(The author is an Associate Professor at the
Graduate School of Social Work, University of Denver)

Dear Editor:

I would like to reply to the published response on my article "Do the Right Thing," in the Summer 1996 edition of your journal. I am a 30 something Caucasian female from Italian American decent. I consider myself a progressive social worker and I am heterosexual. I establish my identity in this way to incorporate the stereotypes about what some readers thought I as the author was or wasn't. More than a few persons, upon personal face to face introduction with me later remarked they were surprised at who I was. They had assumed I was older, probably Hispanic or African American and maybe lesbian. Such assumptions and stereotypes are learned behavior which I raise as an issue for colleagues to think about who and what we think our clients are as well as those who help them. The role of race, class, and gender is poignant in many aspects of my article.

First and foremost while I understand the critical debate seems to lie around my actions, it appears to reframe the real issue which is human rights and dignity for the disempowered. Instead of discussions about me, why are we not, as a profession, responding to the women who may be dying of AIDS in prison? The things I personally saw, felt, and experienced were impossible to forget and necessary to remember.

I personally continue to see the issue of my behavior as one of advocacy. It is no secret we have lost our roots as a profession in the battle between political/ social reform and clinical therapy. I think Harry Specht (1994) had referenced this ideal superbly in *Unfaithful Angels: How Social Work Has Abandoned Its Mission.* (N.Y: The Free Press). However, I don't think it needs to be one or the other. Clinical social workers have direct client contact and a wealth of knowledge to actively participate in social reform. The real question is why we don't and why we have formed two dichotomous camps finger pointing at the other. It remains my opinion, if we are not actively working for change through social action and organizing, we're on the other side and are disloyal to our professional heritage.

Are we to always accept societal laws and do as we're told without question? Do we support the teachings of Dr. King or Malcom X? Civil Disobedience is often at a price but individually and collectively these decisions must be made. We must humanize the dehumanized as our mission.

Finally, I believe many of my critics (published and unpublished) have difficulty with an issue no one has raised: the population! Sadly, homosexuality is uncomfortable for some in our profession. Couple this with reactionary sentiments from the right re: individuals who are incarcerated and their status reduced to subhumans lacking all rights.

Sometimes from sheer exposure, social workers become numb to the lives we intersect with. Sometimes from lack of exposure, we forget the faces and circumstance behind the policies. As Kathleen Powell so eloquently states in her article ("Joshua's Story," *Reflections,* Winter 1996), perhaps it is a basic social work principle to understanding client experience by having to ask for help ourselves. The injustices against people perpetrated through current practices demand a response from Progressives concerned with social well being. We can only make the response reality if we continue to individualize and name our clients to open the eyes of those who cannot or refuse to see the uncomfortable sights, sounds, and smells of disempowered people.

Yes, I am young, it is true.
I don't remember when Dr. King
marched & Malcom went to prison. I
don't even remember the assassination
of President Kennedy or when Mrs.
Parks sat down on the bus.

But YOU remember,
I know you do.

For it is your experience
(perhaps you've forgotten);
but it is my history.
Smuggling condoms & dams into
prison so women don't die of AIDS.

You called it contraband and said I
didn't understand.

This is my experience!

What would you suggest my genera-
tion give the next as their history if not
this?

Sincerely,
Annie L. Houston, LCSW-C,
ACSW

ON THE RECEIVING END OF SOCIAL WORK SERVICES

4

by Marcia B. Cohen, Ph.D.

Marcia B. Cohen, Ph.D.,
Professor, School of Social
Work, University of
New England, Biddeford, Maine.

This narrative chronicles a family tragedy which served to transform my understanding of social work. My years of experience as a social work practitioner and educator failed to prepare me to be a recipient of service. I never knew what it felt like to be a client until my father committed suicide.

OVERTURE

Some months ago I had a painful but profound experience. Painful because it involved the untimely death of my father. Profound because it gave me a significantly deeper and more intuitive understanding of social work.

One Thursday morning in January, I received a phone call from my step-mother, Peg, informing me that my father had jumped ten stories from the balcony of their New York City apartment to the sidewalk below. Miraculously, he had survived the fall, which had been partially broken by the branches of a tree. My father had been rushed by ambulance to the emergency room at Mercy Hospital, just several blocks away. He was in the process of being admitted. Peg was calling his three children, as well her own daughter Eleanor, so that we could come to New York as soon as possible.

By the time I got to New York (the cab ride from LaGuardia Airport predictably taking longer than the plane ride from Maine), it was almost evening. I went straight to the hospital where my father had finally been admitted to the intensive care unit. Apparently everyone—from the police, paramedics, and ambulance drivers to the nurses and doctors—was amazed that a 74-year-old man could have survived such a fall. The news was far from good, however. My father's body was badly broken; he had sustained multiple, severe injuries and was paralyzed from the chest down. During his brief periods of consciousness, he had begged and pleaded with the paramedics, the nurses, the doctors, his wife to allow him to die.

My father, a retired professor of some renown, had a long history of depression. Most of his life the depression was in remission, never really interfering with his professional career. Although earlier depressive episodes had consistently failed to responded to medication, they had always been vanquished by electro-convulsive therapy (ECT). This most recent episode had been different. My father had been severely depressed for well over a year, increasingly unable to speak on the phone, read, or even concentrate on television. All of the myriad new anti-depressant medications that had become available since his previous depressions had been tried. None had any impact on his deepening despair. Finally, the doctors again resorted to ECT. This time, however, my father's depression proved more powerful than electro-shock. There was no improvement. By year's end, there seemed little reason for optimism. He had clearly given up.

FIRST MOVEMENT

When I arrived at the ICU, I saw my own fears and sense of horror reflected on the faces of my family members. The patient in the bed was unrecognizable. He was barely conscious, heavily sedated, and bandaged up to the neck. He was attached to a respirator. A monitor displayed his vital signs in neon purple, yellow, red, and blue. Tubes were taking liquids out of his body. Other tubes were putting different liquids in. I had worked as a hospital social worker for many years. The various technological paraphernalia, their constantly shifting lines and periodic beeps, did not really faze me. My father's appearance did. I was told that the attending physician was expected shortly.

The doctor, a Jewish man in his mid-sixties, was brusque and authoritative. He directed most of his comments to my father's wife, despite her stated preference that he speak with all of us. The bottom line was that my father was lucky (!). He would most likely survive his "fall," albeit as a permanent quadriplegic. I thought to myself, "This is the ultimate nightmare, to be severely depressed and want only to die but without the physical ability to make it happen." A glance of understanding passed between my sister, Sara, and me. I think this was the moment where we both stopped hoping for my father's recovery.

The doctor was still issuing pronouncements. My father would be scheduled for a major surgical procedure to stabilize his back, probably the following week. This surgery would not improve his overall condition but it would enable him to be sat up and fed, making it possible for him to be cared for at home with around the clock help. We were told that the surgeon would meet with us the next day to further discuss the surgery. We raised the question of whether surgery so soon was really such a good idea, but the doctor merely repeated his statement that the surgeon would be speaking with us. Having had little input into that consultation, we sought out the chief resident, an Asian woman in her twenties. Her demeanor was considerably more empathic than the attending physician's. She seemed to understand our growing confusion about the efforts to save my father's life, given his condition, when he had been so specific about his desire to end it. Despite her apparent understanding, there seemed to be nothing she was willing or able to do to intervene. She repeated the mantra that the surgeon would stop by tomorrow afternoon to answer our questions.

SECOND MOVEMENT

Friday morning found Sara, my half-brother, Simon, and me having breakfast at the coffee shop near the hospital. Peg and my step-sister, Eleanor, were at my father's bedside, maintaining the vigil. For the first time, my father's three children gave voice to the unspeakable: Should my father be kept alive when he wanted so much to die? Shouldn't we, who knew better than anyone never to cross him, respect his final wishes? The doctors and nurses were mobilizing all their efforts toward keeping my father alive. Was this what we wanted, or should we persuade them to allow him to die? Couldn't we, as his family, refuse medical treatment on his behalf? Otherwise, what kind of a miserable life sentence were Peg and my father in store for?

We knew we had to talk all this over with Peg as soon as possible, to let her know what we were thinking and gauge her reaction. We needed to include Eleanor in the discussion as well. The topic of allowing my father to die felt scary just to talk about, even among the three of us. We had initially experienced an enormous sense of relief upon learning that his suicide attempt had been unsuccessful. Our first reactions were similar, "Oh please, let him survive this!" It seemed as though many days had passed since we had first received the shocking news...actually, it had been about 24 hours. I awaited the discussion with Peg with considerable trepidation.

We spent the rest of the morning in the hospital, watching the respirator breathe for my father. At lunchtime, we went back to the apartment. I don't remember which one of us first broached the subject of allowing my father to die. Neither Peg nor Eleanor seemed shocked that we had been discussing this. Perhaps they had had a similar conversation. Peg took seriously my father's wish to end his life, although she was clearly uncomfortable talking about hastening his death. She said, in a strained voice, "You all have to remember, I am the one who will have to live with this decision on a daily basis. I need time to think it over, and I need to talk to him about it." She also wanted to discuss the situation with an old and trusted family friend, a physician who had been my father's closest friend since childhood.

We returned to the hospital after lunch and met with the surgeon, another aging white man. At one point in the discussion, Peg interrupted the doctor's detailed description of the planned surgical procedure and questioned its necessity. She explained that her husband had been so depressed and so determined to end his life that she was beginning to question the elaborate efforts to keep him alive. The surgeon acknowledged that he would probably be asking the same questions if this was his family member but that the hospital had legal and ethical obligations to keep my father alive. He did mention several possible courses of action for her to consider and clarified that either her or my father's consent would have to be obtained before any surgical procedure could be done.

Friday evening, Peg called my father's childhood friend and filled him in on what was transpiring. He strongly supported the idea of allowing my father to die. He urged Peg to act immediately in informing the hospital staff of the family's preferences, warning her that they would initiate all kinds of heroic measures if she did not. He assured her that this was the right thing, the caring thing to do for my father.

Peg returned from the phone call galvanized. It seemed as though she had wanted to make this decision all along but had needed support and encouragement from several quarters to convince herself that it was the right decision, motivated solely by concern for her husband. She still wanted to talk to him, if possible, and make sure he had not changed his mind, but she acknowledged that he had made his preferences very clear. The rest of us were relieved, if a bit stunned by the rapidity of her decision. We agreed to persuade the hospital staff to cease their efforts to "save" my father. For the first time in 36 hours we had a plan, a purpose. We knew that we would get resistance from Mercy Hospital and its staff, but we would proceed as a united front.

Things were moving so quickly, I felt dizzy and faintly nauseated. I walked out onto the balcony from which my father had jumped, a place I had been consciously avoiding. I needed to be alone with my thoughts for a little while. I felt strangely close to my father standing out on the balcony, still very sad but calmer than I had felt all day. I marveled at my family's uncharacteristic unity; it was extremely reassuring. I felt convinced we had made a good decision, we were doing the right thing. After a while, the frigid January air sent me shivering back into the warmth of the living room.

THIRD MOVEMENT

Early Saturday morning, we went, en masse, to the hospital. My father was still heavily sedated and seemed unaware of our presence. We asked that the attending physician be paged. Fortunately, he was already in the hospital and came within the hour. Peg spoke firmly of our resolve to allow my father to die and detailed our family friend's specific instructions (including canceling the surgery, removing the respirator, and signing a "Do Not Resuscitate" order). The doctor became annoyed, said he could not remove the respirator until my father could breathe on his own, and indicated that he would have to consult the hospital's attorneys and medical ethics board before considering our requests further. He left the room abruptly. Peg looked deflated. Nothing would or could happen until after the weekend. Ethics boards? Lawyers? This was all getting much too complicated and we had no one in our corner. I suggested we contact the social work department first thing Monday morning. My family agreed.

Needing an excuse to leave the hospital, I volunteered to go to the supermarket to replenish our supplies. When I returned to the hospital, my family was gathered around yet another physician, a white-coated, Caucasian woman in her early forties. Her demeanor, affect, and communication seemed completely different from that of the other doctors. She was commenting on how much strength it must have taken for us to come to our decision, how much we clearly supported each other and wanted what was best for the patient. She concluded the discussion by saying that she would try to help us get through to the attendant or find other members of the medical staff who would be more sympathetic to our position. She left, saying she would be in the hospital and reachable by page all day. I stood just outside their circle, amazed. When she left I exclaimed "That doctor was wonderful, who was she?" Sara replied "She isn't a doctor, she's the social worker." Recognition dawned. The white coat and Saturday work schedule had obscured what now seemed obvious to me. Of course she was a social worker!

CRESCENDO

I raced down the hall and caught up with the worker, introducing myself and my social work credentials. She identified herself as Diane Rivers, a worker at Mercy Hospital for six years. We chatted a bit. She spoke openly about Mercy Hospital's squeamishness about my father's case. Apparently, there was already much concern among the lawyers and higher level administrators. I expressed surprised that they even knew about the situation so soon. She explained that the phones had been humming all morning; this was apparently a very new situation for this Catholic hospital. She saw the hospital as having a long way to go in understanding the many meanings of mercy.

Diane asked me a few questions about my family, reiterating her earlier comments about our strengths. She shared her observation that from our appearances, my siblings and I were presumably the progeny of several marriages. I briefly described our family structure and its complexities. I shared my realization of the previous evening that the current crisis seemed to be bringing us closer together than we had ever been. She told me she often saw that happen in medical emergencies, that this could be something important to build on. The conversation turned to the problem at hand, the resistance of the hospital system to carry out our wishes. Diane told me that a psychiatric consult had been ordered to determine my father's competency to refuse medical intervention and gave me the name of the psychiatric resident she thought would be most sympathetic to our plight. She said she would try to arrange to have this resident assigned to my father's case. She also repeated some of the suggestions she had made to my family in terms of overall strategy and renewed her commitment to advocate for us. She handed me her card, looked me in the eye, and left.

I sat down, letting waves of intense feeling wash over me. I felt understood, appreciated, and valued. I also felt bolstered, respected, and acknowledged as an individual and as a member of a viable, self-determining family unit. I felt joined in the battle against the bureaucracy. Finally, someone shared our perception of the situation and was on our side. Moreover, this was not just anyone; this was someone with perceptivity, training, experience, and knowledge of the hospital system, someone with some clout. I returned to my father's bedside, feeling clearer and stronger.

FINALE

Events followed quickly. The psychiatric resident appeared but was unable to rouse my father. She took the family into a private room and interviewed us at length. Seemingly convinced of our unity and our desire to do what was best, she recommended that the attendant place a "Do Not Resuscitate" order in the chart. The attendant was paged and conferred privately with the psychiatric resident. The attendant apparently was still uncomfortable acting solely on the family's wishes. He wanted to again try communicating with my father, who had not had any pain medication for a while. He shook and shouted at my father and finally managed to rouse him. My father briefly opened his eyes. The attendant ascertained that my father seemed to know where he was and why. He asked my father to blink once if he wanted medical care withheld, if he did not want help to remain alive. My father blinked once, unmistakably. I felt the tension ease out of my shoulders. There was no further productive communication but the attendant seemed satisfied. He explained to us and to the psychiatric resident that he just had to be absolutely certain before he could withhold medical treatment since that went so deeply against the grain of his training and experience.

The attendant wrote orders for my father to be weaned from the respirator and for a "Do Not Resuscitate" order to be placed in the chart. There would be no surgery. Other minor procedures that had been ordered were cancelled. My father would be given nourishment, hydration, and pain medication, nothing else. The doctor warned us that he might continue to live like this for several weeks. Once off the respirator, he would be moved out of the Intensive Care Unit.

Diane stopped by before leaving the hospital for the day to see if we needed anything. We discussed the day's events. She let us know that this had been a pretty big deal for the hospital, that they had been concerned not just about medical ethics but also about potential lawsuits from one or more family members should we come to regret our decision and blame each other and the hospital. We had apparently impressed the psychiatric resident and the attendant as to our unity and resolution. My father's ability to communicate his wishes directly to the attendant had, of course, been pivotal. Diane suggested that we remember this if we should ever question our own decision making, since the final decision had indeed been his. We thanked her for all of her help during this very difficult and exhausting day.

The next day, Sunday, my father was weaned from the respirator. The "Do Not Resuscitate" order was placed prominently in his chart. Sunday afternoon, he was moved to a semi-private room where he was kept heavily sedated on pain medication, which had the side effect of suppressing his respiration. Monday night, my father experienced severe respiratory distress and died.

CODA

One of the few positive aspects of this terrible ordeal was my experience as a social work client. Why did this very brief encounter with the hospital social worker feel so powerful? She was highly competent but really not all that unusual. I had utilized similar skills in my own practice with clients and I had taught hundreds of students to practice, as she did, from an empowerment-oriented perspective. Diane embodied the social work values and skills I had been teaching and preaching for many years: tuning in starting where the client is, conveying empathy, identifying and working with strengths' providing information, mobilizing resources, and offering to intervene on the client's behalf while acknowledging and building on the expertise of the client system. She moved easily between the roles of supporter, clarifier, educator, advocate, and change agent.

As client, I experienced these skills and attributes in a profoundly different way than I ever had as practitioner, teacher, or researcher. What had previously been a series of concepts and constructs became a lifeline, a source of help, a promise of partnership. I gained a very special understanding that weekend of what social work could be.

Some time after my father's death I wrote a letter to Mercy Hospital's Director of Social Work. It read, in part, as follows:

> ... those days were among the most difficult my family has ever faced. Trying to advocate for my father and for ourselves with various medical personnel proved enormously difficult at a time when we were feeling vulnerable and in need of no additional challenges. We were confused, overwhelmed, and frightened.

In the middle of this nightmare, Diane Rivers appeared. The rapidity and accuracy with which she assessed the situation, grasped the complexities of our family composition and dynamics, and tuned into our needs was breathtaking. She understood that we needed support rather than clinical intervention, information rather than answers. She heard our frustration, respected our concerns, and advocated for us with the staff. She also provided us with the necessary knowledge in order to advocate more effectively on our own behalf. In short, Diane's skilled interventions made an unbearable situation significantly more endurable. We finally had someone who was on our side, who understood what we were going through, and whom we could trust ... After a quarter of a century as a social work practitioner and academic, I thought I understood social work practice as well as anyone, but I had never before been on the receiving end. I now realize how different experiencing social work is from that vantage point. Diane helped me to see social work from a wholly new perspective that I cannot adequately put into words. It has to do with the incredible relief and groundedness you feel when your whole world has suddenly turned upside down and you finally discover someone who understands and is on your side, someone who respects what you want and is able to help...

BERTHA REYNOLDS' MEETING WITH PRESIDENT NIXON: THE LOST TAPE.

Paul Abels

Professor Emeritus,
California State University,
Long Beach, CA

I came across the tape in the process of doing an article on Nixon and the Guaranteed Income legislation he was thinking of supporting. He had invited a number of social welfare leaders including Bertha Reynolds to a series of meetings. I could not find any reasons for his asking her, and I must surmise he wanted a cross section of views, and by then, although a radical, she was an elder stateswomen, honored by Smith College, and considered safe.*

It had not been my intention to write about her, until it dawned on me that her conversations were of historical significance to our field, timely, and spoke to current concerns. Her ideas also could have been in response to President

---

*This article is a fantasy. It is almost certain that President Nixon never met Reynolds. The only truths in this article are the words of Bertha Capon Reynolds, and the incidents in her life.

Clinton's efforts to reform welfare, For example at one point she says,

> It looks as if the great undertaking which we call social work is reflecting both society's concern for people in need and the wish of powerful groups to profit by such conditions as an acute shortage of houses or a surplus of unemployed labor. We have noted that the interests which oppose really constructive social work constitute only a small minority of the whole population, but influence a much larger sector through their ownership of newspaper chains and control of radio (TV) broadcasting. . . . Social workers know that it is not the small percentage of the national budget which goes for schools, hospitals and social services which should give us concern, but why it is that a hundred times as much goes for military expenditures which ultimately mean destruction of human life. (In 1996 congress sought to dramatically increase the military budget beyond Pres. Clinton's request).

I had heard something about Reynolds, even read one of her books once when I started teaching social work. I remembered that she was politically astute, had been accused of being a leftist and had been denied employment because of her writings opposing to certain governmental policies, and to some of the directions she saw our profession taking. She was concerned that social workers were in positions where they had to support government/agency policies that might be detrimental to the best interests of the clients, and neglected the basics of a just society and contrary to the mission of our profession. Research which I did later supported some of those recollections, for example she wrote, ". . . people who live under economic handicaps are not free to protest, they are blacklisted as 'trouble makers' and ruled out of such essentials as jobs, living quarters, and a chance to eat" (1963, p. 265.) (An example of "subjugated knowledge," long before it was written about by Foucault.)

To some, she was seen as a "trouble maker" and at times, that carried a painful price. She was barred from study at a seminar she had previously been accepted for after the announcements of a paper she was to give was circulated, the title "McCarthyism vs. Social Work" On another occasion she wrote of her belief that her views kept her from being hired at the Red Cross in 1942, war time, and they were desperately seeking staff. Earlier, she had been forced to leave her position at Smith College because of her ideas and activities. She had been there for fourteen years. Many of her speeches and writing were often critical of the profession, which she dearly loved and was dedicated to, but she feared its moving away from the greater social struggles.

> The way we do our professional work contributes inescapably to the outcome of that struggle. If we think social work is not a force in the battle of ideas, the enemies of the people know better. Either we serve the people's need or we evade them. Either we make democracy real or we reduce it to an abstraction which the foes of democracy do not object to at all. Either we use all that science can teach to help people to build a genuinely good life for themselves, or we build a professional cult that takes the place of interrelations with other advances in human knowledge.

She noted that the speech "did not add to my popularity either with leaders in social work or with some of my colleagues who were personal friends" (1963, pp. 283–4).

When I read her comments about the reactions to her speech, I was reminded of Harry Specht who wrote *Fallen Angels,* and the negative reactions to him personally from some professionals, particularly those devoted to private clinical practice. The issues may change, but the isolation afforded those who remind us of the root purpose of our profession appears to repeat itself, but back to the tape!

She was in support of services that would provide more autonomy for the client. At one point she said . . . "Slowly but surely if we read rightly the signs of the times, there is a melting away, in the thinking of both clients and administrators, the belief that to have to receive relief puts a man in a position in which "beggars must not be choosers" and in which the surrender of self determination is the price of assistance." (1934, p. 31). Of course when she made that statement, the push to force welfare recipients to work had not been a major factor, nor had there been a major push to reform welfare by forcing mothers of small children into the work place. In fact the emphasis during the 70's was to provide assistance so mothers could be home to raise their children.

Someone on the tape raises a question . . . you speak of self-determination; do clients want self determination or is this just some social work idea? Reynolds gave an interesting response, surprising perhaps.

> Self determination is thought by the social case worker to be an essential condition of growth toward maturity of personality but it may not be desired by the client either in itself or as a step toward a goal for which he has no conscious wish . . . some case workers will begin to try to force their clients to be self determining and to

punish them in some way if they do not at least "make a little
noise like" a self determined being. . . . Until we can see that
self-determination for a given client may mean manifestation of
extreme childish dependence because that is the expression of his
choices at the moment, we have not begun to grasp the meaning of
the term but are merely determining, ourselves, how independent
he should be and trying to force him to that norm by our will, not
his (1951, p. 38.)

Do clients want self-determination? Our knowledge of emotional
life admits a double answer: like everyone else they do and they do
not. As long as life lasts, human beings are forced to find some balance between the desire for protection, security, freedom from
struggle and the desire to be individual, to have new experience,
control conditions, make decisions and take responsibility Social
case workers tend to throw their influence to one side or the other
of the struggle. Is it not conceivable that their function might be to
help the client to work out a balance of his own, more satisfying to
him than what he had come upon before and more adapted to his
successfully becoming a part of a social group (1951, p. 39.)

She was a strong believer in individualizing the client, and she
realized just how difficult a task this was for the profession. . . . This
was brought home for me when I read an article she wrote in 1937 in
The Family. She had been asked to help staff of an agency deal with the
extra difficulties staff had in working with "Negro" clients; they missed
more appointments, were late, dropped out etc. Staff believed this
reflected special personality shortcomings.

The question was whether this group could be served, and how
best to serve them, or were special kinds of services necessary.
Reynolds' approach was an example of good practice research, an
approach that might now be called action research. She framed a number of questions to explore including:

1. Are there difficulties peculiar to "Negro" cases, or only more
   frequent and possibly more persistent than other cases?
2. If the difficulties with "Negro" cases are said to be greater, with
   what groups are they compared? How do we find a group that
   is similar so our judgements can be grounded?
3. If factors are related to racial characteristics, what is a "Negro"
   case?

In exploring these and other questions, she provides the staff, and
now the reader with the importance of understanding a group, examining

one's biases, the need for fair comparisons, and important clues in delivering service to groups which may differ from the worker and the usual agency clients. Again we see her advanced thinking, the use of comparison groups became a basic staple for Glasser and Strauss' grounded theory and for comparative approaches. If there is anything she wrote that showed how far ahead of the times she was, it was this series of articles, entitled "A Way of Understanding."

In conclusion she writes

> ... a staff is greatly enriched by having in its membership as much variation in background and points of view as possible, and that it is advantageous to have workers of different races and nationalities provided the following considerations are kept in mind: that such workers shall not be sought as a means of delegating parts of the work which other staff members have found difficult or irksome, and that they shall be chosen for the same personal qualities and given the same opportunity for training as have been found essential for high grade work anywhere. (1931, p. 292)

Once again her writings rang true, as I recalled an article entitled "On Creating a Company of Unequals" which deals with an agency in which clients are assigned a worker, not by need of the client but by the desires of the staff for status, the psychiatrists seeking the most verbal, single problem cases, usually middle class. Psychologists and social workers select next, and the aides, the least trained, being assigned the multi problem cases, usually poor, often ethnic clients.

She understood that the society of the day was involved in a class struggle, and hoped to avoid it in agencies, as the tape reveals she felt the battle was still on she notes "For a social worker to deny that there is a class struggle today is to confess to an ignorance of what is going on. As opportunities to know beat more insistently upon our ears, each day such an unwillingness comes more and more to mean participation on the side of maintaining privilege and exploitation with all its frightful toll of human life" (1935, p. 7). There may have been an additional statement here, but there seemed to be a gap in the tape of about half a minute. One might assume that there might have been a reference to the current administration.

Reynolds' concerns about status and power carried over to her ideas about teaching. "The aims of an education . . . go back to the simplest principles we know—respect for the learners, not as receptacles but as human beings, stimulation to growth, cultivation of sound and fine relationships between individuals and within and among groups, understanding of the dynamic interplay between what we are and do and the social forces of the day" (1942, p. 230). She helped teachers understand the natural learning process by suggesting a five step process from fearful beginner to ability to teach others what one has learned. It helped the teacher to individualize the learner and to reflect on the nature of the teacher/learner relationship. Reynolds firmly believed in the importance of helping people make connections with others, their institutions, and with themselves.

The final portion of the tape deals somewhat with her views on administration. She appears to be discussing her views on what a good administrator might be like. Unfortunately it was at this point where large number of erasures make interpretation impossible. So perhaps I will just conclude with another statement she had made earlier in the session.

> It would be needless to say (were it not too often contradicted by our practice) that if we really believe that life is for growth we shall use no methods that in themselves hamper the growth of the human spirit. We cannot take people by the throat and say "Do as I say and you shall grow." We cannot help them to live coopera- tively with others if we ourselves are not willing to submit to the self-discipline necessary for cooperation with the laws of growth. (*The Family.* Dec. 1935 p. 236)

Her work lives on in her writings, the numerous references to her in the literature, the presentation of her ideas in the classroom, and in the Bertha Reynolds Society, with numerous chapters throughout the country and its annual meeting. It would be interesting to imagine what Reynolds would have to say about the current efforts to dismantle pro- grams she had so vigorously fought to establish.

On one hand she might say it was bound to happen as the power structure would not want to relinquish any of its control or power, and that the capitalist class society had very little concern about the people. On the other hand, of course she would be writing and marching and prodding her colleagues to action. If there were secret tapes with President Clinton, she might very well have told him that his support of the current welfare reform was a direct rejection of the things the Democratic party stands for, and might question his moral fibre. She would also acknowledge his positive actions. It is possible she might even have preferred the efforts that President Nixon made to at least provide everyone with some level of guaranteed income.

REFERENCES

Reynolds, B.C. (1931). "A Way of understanding". *The Family*. Vol. 12 Nov., Dec. and Jan. 1932.

——(1934) "Between Client and Community." Smith College Studies. September.

——(1935) *Social Work Today*. Vol 2. May.

——(1951) *Social Work and Social Living*. N.Y. Citadel Press.

——(1942) *Learning and Teaching in the Practice of Social Work,* N.Y. Russell and Russell.

——(1954) "McCarthyism vs Social Work" Paper delivered at the National Conference of Social Work.

——(1963) *An Unchartered Journey*. N.Y. Citadel Press.

LIVE UNTIL THE FIRST DAY OF THE MONTH

6

By Linda McLellan and Larry W. Foster

Linda McLellan, MSW, is
Oncology Social Worker,
Cleveland Clinic, Cleveland, OH
Larry W. Foster, Ph.D., is Associate Professor, Department
of Social Work, Cleveland State University, Cleveland, OH.

This narrative reflects on a paradigm case for understanding how in an era of managed care when values and economics appear so indivisible, one health care team united and provided non-costworthy care to a terminally ill patient who needed to live until the first day of the month. The ethical dilemma of treatment effect vs. treatment benefit in end of life decision making becomes a drama. The narrative chronicles events leading to the first day of the month and underscore the power of story and metaphor in creating common ground and common understanding in patient care.

THE START

During the middle of a staff meeting, my pager went off. I promptly answered because it was to a number I recognized. It was Dr. Z, a prominent staff oncologist. He said "I have a patient I want you to see." My heart beat a bit more quickly; not once in the four years that I had worked in oncology social work had Dr. Z consulted me directly. In a polished but firm voice he said that he was transferring his patient (Mr. B), who was actively dying, to the oncology service to which I was assigned. Before I could utter a word Dr. Z asserted that he could no longer "ethically" care for Mr. B, who was asking to be kept alive for financial reasons. "Financial reasons?" I asked. Dr. Z mumbled something about an insurance policy. Before I could inquire further, he asked me to meet with Mr. B and his wife to help them be more reasonable in their requests. I realized that this consult was more than to help a family cope with an impending death. My heart sank. "What a setup! If I don't convince this man to accept Dr. Z's recommendations, then what?" At first I felt defensive, then protective of Mr. B. Curious to learn more about the case's history I hurried to the floor, reviewed the chart and met with Mr. B and his wife.

Mr. B was 51 years old and terminally ill with metastatic lung cancer. He had been admitted on the 22nd day of the month with respiratory distress and bone pain. Mr. B was on medical disability from his job of 2 years with a car manufacturer and would not be fully vested in his retirement benefits until the first day of the month; if he died before then all benefits due his wife would be drastically reduced. Mr. B's wife had never worked outside the home and he was worried about what would happen to her if she did not have his insurance benefits to rely on after his death. Despite aggressive treatment Mr. B's respiratory-condition had continued to deteriorate. On the third day of Mr. B's hospitalization Dr. Z had recommended comfort care only; he told Mr. B, his wife, and two young adult daughters that the cancer was terminal and attempts to prolong life would be futile. Rejecting Dr. Z' s recommendation, Mr. B was adamant that he had to live until the first day of the month, even if it meant being put on a ventilator. But after the first, he wanted the ventilator to be taken off.

DILEMMAS

Would honoring Mr. B's request amount to futile treatment and a waste of hospital resources as implied by Dr. Z? When does a patient have a moral claim to futile or virtually futile health care resources? Was a possible social benefit to Mr. B's surviving family members enough justification to provide what appeared to be medically futile care? If Mr. B were kept alive with ventilator support until the first day of the month, would the team be participating in active euthanasia by withdrawing life-support? I thought, "this could be a nightmare . . . how could everyone involved be in agreement?"

THE SEARCH—COMMON GROUND

After meeting with Mr. B and his wife I met with Mrs. B alone. She expressed the wish that her husband would not worry so much about her; she felt that she would survive one way or another and wished he would just focus on his needs. My heart went out to Mrs. B; she presented a mix of emotions including sadness, frustration, fear, and pride. Squeezing my hand, she said, "My husband has always put taking care of me and our daughters number one . . . if he needs to do this, then I'll support him all the way, but I just don't want to see him suffer." She then broke into tears. We both knew that her husband would die soon and that this would be his last request.

As I left Mrs. B, my mind shifted; I wondered how the receiving oncologist and residents would react to Mr. B's request? I caught up with them on rounds and asked to review Mr. B's case with them. They told me that Dr. Z had already reviewed the case with them and that they had seen Mr. B briefly. Fearing that the team may have already been influenced by Dr. Z, I began advocating for Mr. B. To my surprise the staff oncologist turned to the residents and said, "I'll support you if you think you can keep Mr. B alive five more days . . . but it will take a huge commitment of your time to manage his care that closely. It's your call." Shuffling their feet in hesitation, the residents looked at each other and nodded in agreement that they would give it their "best shot." I felt so relieved that I almost missed hearing one of the residents say that he feared keeping Mr. B alive that long may be a medical impossibility; Mr. B's cardiac and respiratory status was deteriorating rapidly and adequate pain control would only suppress his respiration further.

Later that day, Mr. B's primary resident sought me out to tell me that Mr. B's condition was worsening. Anxiously, he said that he didn't want to have to intubate Mr. B and then be faced be with having to withdraw life-support. Looking directly at me he said, "Please contact Mr. B's employer . . . let's make sure his understanding of his company's regulations are accurate. If it is, then try to persuade his employer to make an exception to the rules." The resident seemed very hopeful, more than I was. But I agreed to give it "my best shot."

After obtaining Mr. B's consent I called his human resource representative who confirmed that Mr. B had to live until the first day of the month to collect fully on his benefits; the representative went on to tell me that he had explained this numerous times to Mr. and Mrs. B. Nevertheless, I asked and then pleaded for an exception to the rules emphasizing that this would relieve the pressure of a time line and free Mr. B to focus on being with his family in his final days. My plea for help did not move the human resource person; bureaucratic and inflexible, he expressed neither compassion nor regret but merely quoted policy. Even more frustrating was the newly uncovered fact that an employee would he totally vested in his/her benefit package after being out for three months on a medical disability which Mr. B had been, but the three months were accrued from the first day of month; Mr. B had stopped work in the middle of the month, so his three months did not start being accrued until the first of the following month. That such a technicality could have such a tremendously negative impact on a person's life seemed so unfair! Next, I called Mr. B's union office to see if someone would advocate for him. Although sympathetic, the union representative said that this was a negotiated contract and that there was nothing he could do to help Mr. B. I was given another corporate office number but that call also was to no avail.

Feeling frustrated, if not inadequate, I reported back to the residents that the corporation was inflexible and indeed, Mr. B had to live until the first day of the month to be fully vested in his benefits. They listened, then vented their frustrations about how absurd such inflexibility was and carried on about bureaucracy in general. One resident said he had been dreaming about buying a particular vehicle made by Mr. B's employing corporation but swore he'd never buy this vehicle now! After expressing their anger and disappointment, it seemed that the residents settled in with renewed resolve to fight to keep Mr. B alive five more days to the first day of the month. Upon recollection, it seemed that the bureaucracy had become the enemy, perhaps a metaphor for death.

THE COUNT-DOWN, FIVE DAYS TO GO:

Day One: As supportive players in Mr. B's story the residents began to tell their own stories in relation to Mr. B's struggle. Mr. B's primary resident shared with me that the same manufacturing corporation had treated his grandfather very poorly years ago and told about how this had hurt his grandparents and his family. I found myself captivated by their sharing of hopes and dreams of having a family and about how they would want to be remembered. The residents also talked about their hope that they could help Mr. B beat the odds stacked against him thus enabling him to leave his family the legacy of a productive life vis a vis his pension, health benefits, and life insurance. I remember being intrigued by the team's conversation, particularly how it seemed to shift from confronting the bureaucracy (as a metaphor for death) to the enduring quality of one's legacy (as a metaphor for life).

Day Two: The nurses' station hummed with activity. In the midst of all this I quietly watched as the residents pulled calculators and poured over lab results and resource books trying to make the minute adjustments that might optimize Mr. B's condition. Throughout the day I observed how they talked frequently and at length with Mr. B and his wife about his condition and their attempts to forestall impending death. It struck me that I had never before experienced physicians relating their technical, medical treatment so directly to a patient's story. As the social worker, it typically is my role to ensure that a patient's voice is heard, that his/her story is not lost among other stories and that the care provided is respectful to the patient's narrative. In Mr. B's case, the residents seemed to he assuming this role; while this was gratifying to observe I must admit it also felt a bit unsettling in terms of my role.

Day Three: The residents and the care team were managing to keep Mr. B viable without putting him in the Intensive Care Unit (ICU); but his room was beginning to look like a mini-ICU with all the respiratory monitoring they were doing. Residents, nurses, and respiratory therapists were constantly strategizing with one another about possible technical interventions that might help keep Mr. B alive. I reflected on the phenomena of the almost military approach to treatment that physicians sometimes take in cancer care, which is often experienced by patients and families as distancing them from their physicians (Sontag 1989). However, in Mr. B's case such strategizing seemed to further unite the team with Mr. B and his family. Just when everyone thought Mr. B was unresponsive, he'd open his eyes and whisper, "What day is it? What time is it?" His will to survive until the first day of the month seemed to energize the residents and the team; they marveled at him and talked with me about how they did not want to let him down. I was amazed at the intensity of their efforts and of the feelings evoked in staff as they worked to keep Mr. B alive. I remember beginning to worry how the staff would cope if Mr. B did die before the first day of month.

Day Four (Second Thoughts and the What-Ifs): Everyone seemed to be getting tired. So close to the goal, but yet so many hours away. So much could happen in the next 48 hours. In contrast to the previous day, the residents seemed to need to talk about whether they were doing the right thing, instead of what they could do clinically. They questioned how far they thought they should go with invasive life-prolonging care, and were worried about how they would handle the situation if Mr. B died just hours or minutes before midnight of the first day of the month. One strategy they came up with, was to make sure that the resident on call the last night of the month knew not to respond to a call from Mr. B's floor until after midnight, unless it was to respond to a prearranged number set up with the nurses. This is just one example of the "what ifs" that the residents faced and processed. The "what ifs" were numerous. What if Mr. B died on the 30th and they falsified the time on the death certificate? Who would catch that? Would they lose their license? Would they be thrown out of the residency program? What if they did have to intubate Mr. B today or tomorrow? Would his wife have to sign a consent form to take him off the ventilator? Would his living will help in facilitating pulling life-supports? What if Mr. B's employer figured out that they had kept him alive just long enough to receive his benefits? Could the corporation deny his wife the benefits then after the fact? I tried to address the "what if's" but they were overwhelming. I just kept reassuring the residents they were doing the best they could and validated all their efforts. It was a day of uncertainty clinically, ethically, and legally. The hours seemed to creep by.

Day Five, The Last Day of the Month: The last day of the month finally came; everyone was on edge and began counting down the hours. Intense, worried, but determined, the residents talked together about what they could do technically to keep Mr. B viable and alive until midnight. They continued to express fear about Mr. B dying before midnight. They also began to express sadness, anticipating that even if Mr. B made it through the day, he would die shortly thereafter. The focus of the medical team began shifting from fighting death to preparing for it and to saying good-bye. There were many good-byes being said on the floor that day; the residents would be switching to other medical services on the first day of the month. Typically, residents celebrate going off the oncology service, but these residents were sad to be leaving. On the floors death is often viewed as a failure, as a defeat. Resident physicians tend to experience the oncology rotation as difficult because there is often so little hope of a cure. In Mr. B's case everyone seemed to accept death as inevitable, including Mr. B and his family, but the negotiated goal was to postpone his death. If successful, the team would have met the challenge of bureaucracy and won the battle against death by preserving the legacy of Mr. B's life.

Now there were only hours left to go. Mr. B's family also began talking about letting go; they believed that Mr. B would let go of the struggle to stay alive after he met his goal. I talked with family members about beginning to anticipate the end. They began actively grieving and arranged to spend the night with Mr. B. Their family minister came to sit with them through the night. When I went home about 5:30 p.m. everyone was settled in for the vigil. That evening it was so hard not knowing what was happening with Mr. B; yet, it seemed inappropriate to call in regularly to the hospital to check on Mr. B's status, so I decided that I just had to wait until morning.

The First Day of the Month: Morning of the first day of the month came. I anxiously called in to the oncology floor. Mr. B was still alive! When I got to the hospital, I saw Mr. B's primary resident; he told me that he switched his schedule around to be on-call for the oncology floor on the last night of the month. He said that he was too nervous to sleep so at 12:05 a.m. he went up to Mr. B's room. He said that Mr. B and his family were crying and celebrating that he had made it, but that it was a bittersweet victory celebration since they all knew that Mr. B would be letting go of his fight to survive now that he had met his goal. After talking with his resident, Mr. B opted not to be resuscitated. He also agreed to a morphine drip to control his pain knowing that this might suppress his respiration and thus hasten death. Respiratory monitoring and all blood work was stopped. On that first day of the month, Mr. B's family took turns staying at his bedside as he gradually became less and less responsive. Mr. B died on the first day of the month at 11:30 p.m. with his wife by his side.

CONCLUDING THOUGHTS

As I reflect on the case of Mr. B today I have renewed appreciation for the extent to which health care professionals contributed from their specific disciplines to Mr. B's care. Also, I am reminded of the power of story and of metaphor in the creation of common understandings in patient care; paradoxically, we health care professionals may have to look upward to find our common ground. As illustrated in the case of Mr. B, unity was found in the metaphors of legacy and bureaucracy— or life and death, respectively. Sharing these metaphors enabled the health care team to acknowledge the vulnerability, strength and inter-dependence of the human spirit in each of us.

　　. . . *We invent stories about the origin and conclusion of life because we are exiles in the middle of time. The void surrounds us. We live within a parenthesis surrounded by question marks. Our stories and myths don't dispel ignorance, but they help us find our way, our place at the heart of the mystery. In the end, as in the beginning, there will be a vast silence broken by the sound of one person telling a story to another. (1989,* Keen & Valley-Fox, *p.128)*

REFERENCES

Keen, S. & Valley-Fox, A.(1989) *Your mythic journey: Finding meaning in your life through writing and storytelling.* Los Angeles: Jeremy P. Tarcher, Inc.

Sontag, S. (1989). *Illness as metaphor and Aids and its metaphors.* New York: Doubleday.

DOING ALCOHOLISM TREATMENT IN NORWAY: A PERSONAL REMINISCENCE

By Katherine van Wormer

Katherine van Wormer, MSSW,
Ph.D., is Associate Professor,
Department of Social Work,
University of Northern Iowa,
Cedar Falls, Iowa

This narrative provides an insider's view of work in a Norwegian alcoholism treatment center, not at a typical center in Norway, but at one modeled loosely (very loosely) on the American 12 Step approach. Because there was a lack of regulation externally and of professionalism internally, this American's experience was fraught with challenges of a most disturbing sort. Although social workers generally will be unable to preserve their ethical integrity in a system dominated by profit and interpersonal conflict, the rewards of speaking out and exposing ethical violations can make even the most unsavory of experiences ultimately seem worthwhile.

Last night I dreamed I was back at Gjovikseter (a fictitious name). The dream was one of those where you are a trespasser on forbidden territory and just about to get caught. Here I was an intruder, and there was no escape; feelings of guilt and shame were overwhelming as I found myself face to face with my former boss, the director. What am I doing here? How can I explain? I beg his understanding and forgiveness, but am ordered away. Even long after the particular images have faded in the light of day, the feelings of disquiet and trepidation continue to hang over me like a cloud.

THE HONEYMOON PERIOD

Perhaps I should start at the beginning. In 1987 I spotted a job ad that seemed too good to be true. "Alcoholism counselors wanted to bring the Minnesota Model to Norway." Being in Minnesota, I was at the right place at the right time. My family was more excited than I was as I went to Minneapolis for what turned out to be a delightful interview. Alcoholism counseling was my field, and though I did not know what the Minnesota Model was, much less how to teach it, my expertise was taken for granted. (This model was AA's Twelve Step program, I later learned.)

From 1988 to 1990 I spent two very exciting and fulfilling years as the treatment director of an alcoholism center. The center was located at a former ski resort on the top of a mountain with a view of the town below that was breathtaking. My role as the "professional in residence" entailed lecturing to clients (including family members) and modeling counseling skills for counselors-in-training—trainees. Trainees doubled as translators and therapists, translating for me and my fellow American colleague, Ed*, as we participated in group and family therapy.

Ed, an AA hard liner, tough on the outside but with a heart of gold, practically ran the place. Ed's charisma and hilarious first-hand stories of his drinking days and reluctant recovery made my contributions seem pale in contrast. What could have been a competitive situation— me with the academic credentials, Ed with the know-how—grew into a relationship of incredible sharing and kidding around and team play. Everything I was to learn about Norwegian culture—the school system, the mistranslation of words, the work norms—I was to learn from this man. I also got to witness some amazing treatment techniques.

---

*All names are fictitious

A motherly figure, the assistant director, Inger, was everyone's caretaker. Her fluency in English, humorous insights, and utter efficiency in managing personal and administrative crises eased my transition into a foreign culture and very strange work atmosphere. "Katherine, this a crazy house," was Inger's constant comment. Much of Inger's frenetic energy, it later became apparent, was consumed with covering up the mistakes of her boss, Kai (pronounced to rhyme with high). A man of great charm, Kai dressed in a sailor jacket and flirted with any woman who trusted him enough to smile. Seeing himself in the role of perpetual victim, Kai was given to describe his feuds with people, men who falsely accused him of owing them money or women who cried out "sex-press" (sexual harassment). Inger's fierce loyalty to the director and to the mission of the treatment center stemmed from her very, very recent experience as a client there. In fact, except for the chef, every member of staff, from the cleaning crew to the director himself, was a recovering alcoholic, some with as little as two months sobriety.

While I was happily adjusting to the carefree schedule of my job—engaging in public relations work, visiting treatment groups, and delivering lectures on group therapy to trainees—Ed was growing more and more frustrated. Standards were declining, he said. Kai was more interested in newspaper publicity (and attracting celebrities to treatment who would be written up in the tabloid press) than in recruiting a professional staff or maintaining professional standards. Especially worrisome to Ed was the lack of required sobriety for trainees who were doing the therapy and relapsing as frequently as the clients, not to mention the frequent violation of clients' confidentiality in the interests of newspaper publicity and the frequent sexual liaisons between clients and staff.

Still, delighted to be living in one of the most beautiful and richest (no poverty in sight anywhere) countries in the world, gratified by the opportunity to help highly educated and well motivated clients, and intrigued by the daily soap opera of life at Gjovikseter, I managed to find a niche for myself. The only slight dampener to my spirits was the polluted physical environment—virtually every person at the treatment center smoked except for Ed and me. Staff meetings grew intolerable as we all got shut in as winter approached.

About this time Ed fell out of favor with the director. The latter took to reminding me that my loyalty must be to him and not to Ed.

Meanwhile, Ed was growing increasingly wary as he watched his power base disintegrate slowly and surely. He confided in me, and only in me, of his misgivings. Staff meetings conducted mostly in English for the sake of "the Americans" grew increasingly hostile and belligerent. Kai, who earlier had ceded much of the decision making to Ed so that he could pursue an intense love affair with a young, former client and ex-prostitute, now, spurned by his lover, moved to regain his power base. Abrupt lower level staff changes followed. Bringing on board his ex-bodyguard and confidant from a rough former life, Kai ordered the program director's translator and right-hand man to a branch center in Oslo. My American colleague now found much to complain about: first there was the ex-bodyguard's—Gunnar's—very recent drinking episode; then there was the director's public involvement with a string of much younger women. Meanwhile, Gunnar, in a pre-trainee status, secretly moved in with the more mature and motherly assistant director, Inger. In the midst of the chaos, my colleague returned to America for a Christmas vacation. Upon his arrival in America, Ed had a stroke and died. He was 50 years old.

THE CULTURAL CONTEXT

A disclaimer at this point may be in order. Events that ensued at Gjovikseter probably say more about the pitfalls of alcoholism treatment, the nature of addiction and addictive relationships than they do about Norway. In Norway, alcoholism treatment ordinarily was provided free of charge by the state. Psychologists led treatment groups; the focus was on individual responsibility and control. The disease model of alcoholism was relatively unknown in the late '80s. Transported from America this model guided treatment at the several private, unregulated treatment centers such as the one which is the subject of this article. Because there was much hostility to privatization in this part of Scandinavia with its shining socialist tradition, the private center operated entirely independently. The director-owner—"the chief alcoholic" as he called himself—answered to no one. In a country in which even the sales of used cars are closely regulated, the operation of this center was a strange anomaly. For a comprehensive view of Norwegian cultural traditions, traditions stressing humanity, equality, and cooperation, see *Social Welfare: A World View* (van Wormer, 1997).

A State Of Inner Turmoil

Several months later, five trainee therapists decided to "blow the whistle" to the press concerning certain unethical practices. Their concern was with the sexual harassment to which they had been subjected, the "kidnapping" of clients into treatment (staff members would get reluctant clients very, very drunk, then drive them up to the treatment center), and the lack of pay for trainees, who were instructed to pretend they were not working so as to qualify for sick pay money from the state. These disgruntled workers, their picture on the front page of Norway's major newspaper, were simultaneously fired. Newspaper headlines chronicled unfolding events such as a near fist fight between Gunnar and the union leader

Then one night, I was summoned to a late night meeting where Gunnar and tearful staff members were coerced into signing loyalty oaths. Only a few of us refused to sign. My speech of opposition to the firings went untranslated. Without any training, Gunnar and Inger, now an obvious couple, ran the treatment program for alcoholics and their families. My role (I was now the program director) was secondary. Somehow, over time, thrown in continual contact, Gunnar, Inger, and I all became friends. It was then that Inger confided in me that Gunnar had physically threatened the late program director just before his departure from Norway. This happened at the airport; Ed had seemed to be in a state of confusion as he boarded the plane. Gunnar had been "under orders" from the director to frighten Ed so badly that he would never come back to Norway. Gunnar now blamed the director as well as himself and was no longer loyal to him. Overcome with guilt, he wanted me to know the whole story.

For guidance, I looked increasingly to professional ideology. Researching the social work code of ethics over and over, I pored over the part about one's professional responsibility to one's colleagues and to the community. Unable to eat (at work) or sleep, my mind began to race forward with possibilities and intrigues. Revenge plots occupied my mind to the point of utter obsession. I refused to sign the letter to the editor written by the remaining staff proclaiming our support for the director. I wrote glowing letters for fired staff members (these documents were later used in court proceedings in which the director was sued for illegal firings); I crashed into an executive conference with bankers and labor leaders to speak on behalf of the recently former staff. I stayed in touch with the fired workers. For the most part, however, although seething within, I acted loyally and friendly on the surface. And I continued to throw myself into addressing the needs of some very appealing and eager-to-learn clients and their families.

With the departure of Ed, use of the English language departed also. Effectively cut off from most communication, I became intellectually and socially isolated. New trainees, recruited from clients who stayed on at the halfway house, spoke only faltering English. Their sobriety was faltering also.

By now I had been in Norway six months. My children were thriving in school and my husband gloried in the delights of a caring community. My inability to speak the language wedded me to the job in what had now become in a literal sense "a crazy house." Inger and I alternated between being close and being caught up on opposite sides of the conflict between the top administration and the fired workers. Paranoia filled the air as the director and Inger sought out enemies of the center. Gjovikseter staff were instructed not to fraternize with former staff. Over a two-year period there were 50 former staff members scattered over Norway and Minnesota.

THE DECISION TO ACT

The dilemma—how to survive in a hostile work environment and how to maintain one's professional integrity while publicly representing an ethically corrupt outfit—was resolved early in the second year of my employment. Unable to simply "turn a deaf ear," I would become a spy. Gathering evidence, I would "come clean," I decided, by releasing this evidence to the public. Fortuitously, the editor of *Sosionomen,* the Norwegian social work journal, called to request an article. The issue was to be the need for regulation of alcoholism treatment centers. Forthcoming in May, the article would be professionally translated into Norwegian. Since I planned to return to the U.S. in June, the timing of the inevitable firing would be manageable.

One of my greatest fears concerning the pending article was my anticipation of utter rejection from Inger and her "sambor'" (partner). As fate would have it, however, both of them were to break up their relationship, completely bum out, and depart well before the appearance of the article. "Kai is a psychopath," they declared. Still not trusting them, I said he wasn't that bad. However, their tales of Kai's earlier life were harrowing. Gunnar's return to his long-forgotten wife left Inger in a state of deep depression that was to persist for the better part of a year. Today, fully recovered, she is happily directing her own treatment center while her former partner has established a successful career as a family therapist in Sweden. Both have quit smoking.

In any case, when the article came out, the very people I dreaded facing were no longer there and were now very supportive. My most immediate problem was to get the promised air fare for myself and my family (a total of $4,000).

When my article "The Need for Regulation" (van Wormer, 1990) hit the press, I was in the process of negotiating the return air fare for myself and my family. Characteristically, Kai had been stalling for weeks. Then all negotiations came to an abrupt end. "You will not get your air fare money now," he said. I had several hours to clear everything out of my desk and office. My salary and holiday money were confiscated. And what a shock when I got to read in the local paper that police charges would be filed for *underslag*—embezzlement!

With the permission of *Sosionomen*, I will cite the whistle blowing portion of that article. The local press highlighted my accusations. This portion chronicles the depth of my professional compromise:

Professionals who work for an organization which engages in questionable practices become necessarily implicated in the carrying out of those practices. Compromise becomes an essential form of survival in the unregulated, profit-oriented treatment institution. The social worker will try to work within the system to change the system and then one day, in anger and desperation, will turn to the outside. . . .

I have survived at this treatment center because as a foreigner [unable to speak Norwegian] I have really had no option. Also, I thought I could have some influence. I have survived by uttering feeble protests, manipulating the situation where possible, but mainly by "turning a deaf ear." I have turned a deaf ear to some of the following practices in which I was directly or indirectly involved:

- Placing recent ex-clients on night watch duty; this entailed distribution of sedative medications.
- Training recent ex-clients to do therapy before they were ready, encouraging them to receive their money illegally from the government.
- The firing of the entire treatment staff (except for the director's ex-bodyguard) for disloyalty to the director.

- Pressing clients to proclaim their illnesses publicly to the press.
- Pulling clients out of treatment to perform duties "for the home."
- Getting clients drunk, then "kidnapping" them to treatment.
- Violation of health laws pertaining to rights of nonsmokers.
- Turning former clients out of aftercare programs for disloyalty.
- Sexual harassment (sex press) of clients and staff. van Wormer (1990)

The aftermath of the article—the confiscation of the money owed me and the false charges made the point better than the article itself. Regulation by the state was necessary to protect whistle blowers as well as the ordinary workers and clients. Writing the article, however, was therapeutic; it was catharsis in the form of revenge—revenge for Ed, the fired trainees, and the dozens of women who were sexually harassed. And now for a universal question: Can a social worker maintain his or her integrity in a treatment center run for the sole purpose of making money? In most cases, no. In a corrupt enterprise, in one way or another, all participants are corrupted.

CONCLUSION AND FINAL THOUGHTS

In the end, thanks to the formidable Norwegian Social Work Union, of which I had not even been a member, I won my case in court. The Norwegian social work organization was deeply shocked at the unprofessional practices going on at such private centers as the one in question. Just recently, Kai was found guilty in a civil case involving sexual harassment of a secretary and ordered to pay her a substantial sum. In his defense, the director was quoted in a newspaper article as saying, "I only touched her in the very best sense of the word," and in a TV interview as proclaiming, "I am impotent so how can I bother anyone?" Reportedly, Gjovikseter continues to thrive and clients continue on their tough road to recovery.

Writing in *The Whistleblower*, a book which provides an in-depth analysis of individuals who speak out against their companies, Glazer and Glazer (1989) quote one of their subjects as follows:

As a whistleblower you will experience every emotion known to mankind. . . . Be prepared for old friends to suddenly become distant.

Be prepared to change your type of job and life style. Be prepared to wait years for blind justice to prevail. Glazer and Glazer (1989, p. 237).

I feel lucky that I arrived in Norway when I did and that I had the professional tools and connections to do what I did. The sadness that haunts me is that when I left, nobody waved good-bye. The joy is that now, several years later, all is forgiven (by my colleagues) and/or understood. Nothing in graduate school prepares us, nothing in the professional journals informs us of how tough it is to fight an organization. To be willing to blow the whistle, you have to be willing to be seen as a traitor. Still, support from a professional association can provide tremendous psychological as well as monetary support. Besides, helping to change the system, a corrupt and damaging system, is one of the most thrilling and meaningful things a social worker can do. But no matter how much self-congratulation there may be in the after years, there are always those haunting dreams. . . .

REFERENCES

Glazer, M. and Glazer, P. (1989). *The Whistleblower.* New York: Basic Books.

van Wormer (1990). The need for regulation. (Behov for regulering.) *Sosionomen* 10: p. 21–23.

van Wormer (1997). *Social welfare: A world view.* Chicago: Nelson-Hall.

BEING A VOICE IN A FOREIGN LANGUAGE

A Commentary on "DOING ALCOHOLISM TREATMENT IN NORWAY: A PERSONAL REMINISCENCE" by Katherine van Wormer

By Dale Weaver, Ph.D.

Dale Weaver, Ph.D., is Lecturer,
Department of Social Work,
California State University,
Long Beach

As a profession, social work is informed by both practice experience and scholarly activity, and effective teachers of social work rely on both academic material and lessons from their own professional careers. In teaching macro practice classes, one of the lessons I pass on from my own turbulent administrative career pertains to assessing for oneself just when decisive, ethical career action is necessary. I tell my students that such action is required when a point is reached at which there is significant disparity among the interests of one's own career, the interests of the agency where one works, and the interests of the population being served. We can call this guide to action the "principle of mutual interests". The application of the principle of mutual interests rests on a clear understanding of the power differences among clients, workers, and agencies.

The initial importance of this principle is to get students to understand that their interests, and the interests of their agencies, are not necessarily congruent with the interests of their clients; in fact, the interests are not expected to always be congruent in the real world. The second important purpose of the principle of mutual interests is to encourage students to continually monitor and evaluate the interests of these three "interest groups." Though it ought to be a simple matter to articulate one's own career interests, it is my experience that few of us consistently do this. Often we assume that by following the dictates of our public-spirited agencies and by concentrating our energies on serving our clients, our careers will naturally prosper. The idea of consciously pursuing our own career interests, possibly at the expense of the interests of others seems unsavory and at odds with the spirit of our profession. In fact, however, one is both less likely to engage in conflicts with the interests of others and more likely to prosper, if one sets clear personal career goals and milestones of achievement on the way to those goals.

Van Wormer was in a fortunate position, that is, understanding her own interests while in Norway. In spite of the difficulty of sorting out these issues in another culture, the length of her stay there was proscribed ahead of time, and her career in the States was not threatened by her actions in Norway. It was her task in regards to her own interests to complete the enjoyable family stay in Norway, resolving issues of professional conscience as she left. She did accomplish this temporal balancing act, though cutting it a bit close, as she lost her air fare home at the last moment.

That the interests of our agencies may be incongruent with the interests of both organizational staff and clients is a truism of administrative theory and practice. Much has been written about "goal displacement" and about the primacy of the need for organizational survival. Again, however, the pursuit of mere organizational survival is a reality which conflicts with the aspirations and world views of social work students. The principle of mutual interests serves as a reminder to social work practitioners of the need to separately consider and evaluate the impersonal interests of our host organizations.

At Gjovikseter no one, with the possible exception of Ed, seemed to be doing that. As described, the agency was little more than a setting for the pursuit of individual interests—professional, financial, and sexual. For van Wormer, the agency was a succession of personal and professional alliances, a system within which she generally felt comfortable, as she was able to establish separate personal and professional relationships with nearly all of the primary actors. However, identifying and articulating the interests of the agency itself, separate from the interests of a tangled web of scheming individuals, may have brought some clarity to the situation.

More troubling, however, in Gjovikseter as described by van Wormer was the lack of overt consideration of client interests. Determining, articulating, and evaluating the best interests of clients is the most difficult of all, because it begs the question of who has the right to speak for clients, and because this action cannot avoid the power differences between clients and helpers. Professionals are quick to appoint themselves the guardians of the best interests of their clients; indeed, professionalism can be defined in terms of the knowledge and values needed to articulate and represent those interests. But this notion of professionalism rests on the assumed right and power of professionals to speak for clients. Accepting the expressed interests of clients on their own terms is a more challenging method of practice. Never failing to consider the interests of clients is perhaps the most important challenge of our profession because of their frequent lack of power to be heard regarding their own interests. The "very appealing and eager-to-learn clients and their families" at Gjovikseter seemed to be receiving effective treatment at times, while having their rights violated at other times. I think that a clear articulation of the interests of clients in this organizational mess would have gone a long way toward clarifying the need for ethical action, as well as the urgency for that action.

How do we know when the need for action has arrived? Frequently, simply when the pain of continued inaction becomes too great. As social workers, when we feel that these moments have arrived, the principle of mutual interests may help us to rationally recognize and assess these moments. Usually, however, there is a simpler way. Professional codes of ethics, government licensing and oversight of professions, personnel policies and practices, and regulatory oversight of non-profit institutions are attempts to achieve a fair balance of interests by reducing the power differences among clients, workers, and agencies. These codes require that professionals do not discount the interests of their clients, and that agencies do not violate the rights of their workers. Hence, clear violations of written and normative professional and institutional regulations are a sure sign that the principle of mutual interests has been transgressed.

It is not clear from the article just when van Wormer felt the need for action. After "the frequent violation of clients' confidentiality . . . , and the frequent sexual liaisons between clients and staff," she was "still delighted to be living in one of the most beautiful and richest countries in the world." In spite of a number of egregious violations of ethical and regulatory guidelines, she remained passive until forced to publicly proclaim her loyalty. The difficulty for her must have come from her status as a cultural outsider. We know that rules are never applied exactly as written; there are always customary informal norms governing the application and timing of formal regulations. How is an outsider to be familiar with these norms? Especially when direct understanding of these norms is cut off through lack of familiarity with the local language. And does an "outsider," a guest in a foreign county, have the same rights, the same obligations to come forward, when the locals around her seem all too comfortable in the face of violations? It is telling that van Wormer turned to a professional code of ethics for guidance rather than to the local regulations governing her workplace, even though there were consistent clear violations of those regulations. "Increasingly for guidance I looked to professional ideology." Was it her status as a cultural outsider which led her to professional norms for guidance? Can a professional code of ethics guide behavior for professionals cross-culturally?

After determining that the present situation is untenable, what courses of action are available to us? Hirschman (1970) tells us that dissatisfied organizational members have three options for action, expressed in the title of his classic work, *Exit, Voice, And Loyalty.* In choosing exit, we avoid the conflict by leaving the situation and going on to another; voice means that we remain in our positions and work openly to resolve the conflict; and expressing loyalty means that we remain in the situation no matter what, tacitly accepting the violation of interests. Our choice of option depends on our assessment of the viability of the options and our own alternatives. Choosing exit implies generous career alternatives to the present situation. Choosing voice implies a belief in the possible effectiveness of this option, an investment in the present situation, and possibly the presence of alternatives if one is forced to exit. Choosing loyalty implies few alternatives and a belief that expressing oneself will not be effective.

Van Wormer"s status as a visitor constrained the exit option in a unique way. While, as she stated, "my inability to speak the language wedded me to the job . . . ," at the same time her departure from the job was predetermined. "Since I planned to return to the U.S. in June, the timing of the inevitable firing would be manageable." So, while exit was not immediately feasible, it was a certainty in the near future. Generally, this is the organizational situation not of regular employees, but of consultants or of employees on limited contracts. At the same time, her status as a visitor precluded the need for a deep or extended loyalty to the agency. She needed only to ". . . find a niche for myself." Indeed, her loyalty was to a succession of organizational actors, rather than to the agency itself.

Due to the constraints on her exit and loyalty options in this situation abroad, this chapter is a wonderful description of the voice option in the face of the need for decisive action, in particular the frustrations of exercising the voice option in a foreign land with an unfamiliar language. The first exercise of voice was a negative one and was forced by circumstances, as van Wormer refused to sign a loyalty oath. Her first proactive voice articulation was negated. "My speech of opposition to the firings went untranslated." What a frustration it must be to act, but to not be heard. She went on to refuse to write some letters, while insisting on writing others—manipulating her voice ethically. However, "effectively cut off from most communication, I became intellectually and socially isolated." Again, professionalism guided van Wormer toward action, as a professional journal came forth to finally provide her with an effective forum for her voice. Her voice was effective in that it led to the official regulations necessary to achieve a balance among interests in social service organizations. And the effective exercise of the voice option successfully resolved van Wormer's personal dilemma, as it "was therapeutic, it was catharsis in the form of revenge."

REFERENCES

Hirschman, A. O. (1970). *Exit, voice, and loyalty.* Cambridge, MA: Harvard University Press.

VIOLET'S SEEDS

by Joshua Miller

Joshua Miller is Associate
Professor at Smith College School
for Social Work. He would like to
thank his wife and children
for their support with this project.

This narrative provides reflections by a social worker in mid-career on a painful and significant encounter with one of his first clients in London over 20 years ago. Themes of loss, guilt, trauma are uncovered along with an exploration of the meaning and transformation of a helping relationship.

Sometimes things happen in your life that change you forever—things that were not anticipated or expected. This is such a story.

In the mid-1970's, I received my MSW from the University of Washington and was assuming that I would spend the rest of my life living and working in the splendid city of Seattle. But a professor of mine, Fred Lewin, who had just returned from a year's sabbatical in England, suggested that I try working in London. The English social service system had recently been reorganized to a generic model, administered by local authorities (like counties or boroughs), and most significantly, there was a critical shortage of trained social workers. Fred gave me some contacts to whom I wrote.

I was surprised when the Assistant Director of Social Services for a South London borough wrote back to me, offering me a six month's probationary job, sight unseen. How could I turn this offer down? I was 25, unattached, not yet professionally grounded, and living and working in Europe sounded romantic and exciting. So I figured that I would go and work for a year, do a bit of traveling, and then return to my home in the Pacific Northwest.

Within 6 months my work permit had arrived, clearing me for employment and in a snowstorm on April 1, I departed by Icelandic Air lines to London.

The social service department for the borough was located in a Town Hall that housed a variety of municipal services. My team covered a vibrant township in the borough that housed Africans, East and West Indians, migrants from Ireland, Scotland, and Wales, as well as an ensconced indigenous working class population. There was a thriving High Street, dotted with pubs and Indian restaurants, lined with street vendors animatedly hawking fruit and vegetables.

There were five social workers on the team, two social work aides, a sector clerk, and the team leader, who was a Senior Social Worker. There were an Italian social worker and a German social work aide on the team, and shortly after I arrived, a Swedish social worker, so we were soon nicknamed the "International Brigade." Within a few weeks, I had clients with mental illness, people with physical disabilities, couples suspected of abusing their children, adolescents who had run away or had broken the law, and many homeless people. A caseload averaged between 25 and 40 cases. There were few other social service resources (no community mental health centers, scarcely any social service agencies) so that the local authority social worker was expected to provide everything: case management, counseling, information and referral, advocacy, supervision of custody orders, and groupwork, as well as evaluations for special apartments or equipment for the disabled.

Many of my clients were assigned to me when I was a "duty worker," doing intake for new cases, and many were homeless. There was a severe housing shortage in London at this time, but there was also a statutory obligation to house homeless families with children. Social workers were expected to assess whether or not there was, indeed, a homeless family with children and no other options, and then place the family in a temporary shelter, usually a bed and breakfast hostel. Families waited months, even years, before being offered permanent housing in state owned units known as "council housing."

VIOLET

In early May, I met Violet Johnson while serving as a duty worker. It was a random chance that she became my client. Violet declared herself to be homeless and asked for my help in resettling her and her six children. She was not only asking for help with housing; she was concerned for her life and for the safety of her children.

Violet was an attractive but haggard looking woman in her late 30's. She was dark skinned, with high cheekbones and dark, solemn eyes. She had been born in a West Indian country but had been living in London for about 12 years. Her parents were of African, East Indian, and European descent. There was a mixture of fear, resignation, defiance, and maternal love in her story as she spoke. Her husband, and the father of her six children (aged 5 to 16), had severely beaten her and was at home with the six children. The beating was part of a recurring pattern, and she had finally decided to leave. She was concerned that if her husband found her, he would kill her, and she was also fearful that he would mistreat her six children. However, she was adamant that I should not visit him. Her reasoning was that he would be charming and respectful to me, but he would then take out his anger on the children after I left.

Violet was accompanied by a family friend, Mr. Andrews, who was from the same West Indian country. He confirmed her story and attested to the risks of my visiting Mr. Johnson to check on the children. We worked out a plan. He would visit the house and the children on a daily basis, and I would phone the children's school. I would ask that the Education Welfare Officer visit the home if any of the children were absent. Violet was going to stay with her parents and would stay in contact with me. The plan was for her to collect her children eventually and then to be rehoused in a location where her husband would be unable to find her.

For the next month and a half, Violet lived with friends and her parents. Mr. Andrews visited the home regularly. I phoned the schools on a weekly basis. At my request, the Education Welfare Officer made a home visit and reported that Mr. Johnson is a charming man and that the children seemed to be well cared for. Violet and I would meet on a weekly basis. She had had to leave her job at a government agency because her husband worked there. We discussed her plans to seek new employment, her financial situation, her anguish over her children being cared for by a man whom she viewed as dangerous, and her determination to leave him. She often looked tired and weak, but her will was strong. When she was unable to keep appointments with me, she would send me letters, keeping me appraised of her progress. She eventually consulted a solicitor (lawyer) and took out a summons against her husband for persistent cruelty and sought custody and care and maintenance of her children. She was advised that she could not take out a restraining order against him unless she was first attacked and the police were called to the scene.

A few days after the summons was served, Violet came to my office with her oldest child, her daughter Kate. Kate was a tall, thin 16 year old with short, tightly curled hair. Violet asked Kate to show me some bruises on her chest that she alleged had been inflicted by Mr. Johnson. Kate timidly complied. I saw some dark bruises that could have been inflicted by hard slaps or punches. Earlier that day, Kate had gone to her maternal grandparents' house and had reported how her father had beaten her and her sister Laura.

Violet had immediately gone to the children's schools, removed all of them, and took them to her parents' apartment in an adjacent South London borough. After we consulted with my supervisor, all parties agreed that Violet would immediately go to court and seek custody of the children, rather than have the local authority seek a Care and Protection Order.

Two days later I accompanied Violet to her court hearing. Unable to sit with Violet, I observed the proceedings from the gallery. It was the first time that I had seen Mark Johnson, her husband. He was a tall, handsome, tan skinned man, also originally from the West Indies; he was dressed in a suit. Violet made a deliberate and detailed presentation of their relationship together. They had met and been married in the West Indies. Their three eldest children had been born there before they immigrated to England. She described how he became increasingly violent toward her, often forcing himself on her sexually. When she was pregnant with her fourth child, she was severely beaten by him. The child was born with profound deafness.

Violet described how the violence escalated and was directed toward the children as well as herself. The courtroom was gravely silent as she described being knocked unconscious by Mark and raped in front of the children, and another time being raped with a Coca Cola bottle. I watched Mark as Violet related all this. The left side of his face twitched rhythmically and uncontrollably. I thought to myself, "He can't take this; his self concept doesn't allow for this; he is going to explode." With the exception of the twitching, he stood stoically. The hearing was continued with Violet being granted temporary care and custody of the children.

NIGHT

Two and one half weeks later, Violet was putting her children to bed at about 10 p.m. on the second floor of her parents' apartment. There was a knock at the door. Violet started down the stairs to open it. Kate followed her, cautioning her not to open the door in case it was Mark. Violet reassured her that she would keep the door on the chain to see who was there.

She latched the chain and opened the door. With a tremendous crack, the door flew open, the chain dangling lifelessly. Mark burst in. Violet screamed. The remaining children ran to the top of the stairs and started to scream. Mark slammed Violet's head from one wall to another. Then he pulled out the Stanley knife and hammer head that he had been carrying in his pockets and slashed and beat her. Kate tried to intervene and was cut on her hand by the knife.

Mark dropped Violet's limp and bloody body and said to Kate: "Come with me." He took her by the hand and started to walk down the street with glazed eyes. A few minutes later, a police car pulled up, and Mark was arrested without a struggle. The next day, he was charged with the murder of Violet Johnson.

INNER CITY BLUES

I was sitting at my desk in my team room two days later. We had recently moved out of the gloomy town hall into an area office building that overlooked the High Street. It was a sunny morning, and from my second floor window, I watched a vegetable vendor gesticulating wildly about tomatoes when I took Kate's call. As soon as she identified herself, I felt everything freeze. When she said, "Something has happened to Mom," I still asked her, "What happened?" even though I knew what she was about to tell me.

When I asked Kate if the family would like me to visit that day, she said "Yes." When I arrived, I met all of the children, Violet's parents, Mr. and Mrs. Patel, as well as some family friends, including Mr. Andrews.

Let me briefly describe the family for you. Kate was a very verbal, intelligent 16 year old, an A student and very much the eldest child. Laura, who was 15 at the time, and Sandy, who was one week shy of her 14th birthday, looked more like each other physically, with a strong East Indian influence in contrast to Kate's African features, and were closely aligned with one another. Laura was less outgoing than Kate, more guarded in her demeanor, while Sandy, who looked strikingly like Violet, had a miserable cold and was withdrawn.

Markie was 11, thin, and looked a lot like his namesake, his father. He could barely lip read and was comprehensible only if one stood very close to him and listened attentively. He could not sign. With all of the commotion in the house, he was alert (like a cat listening to rapid noises coming from all directions) but not in direct communication with people. That situation persisted over the next few weeks and, to some extent, for the next few years.

Julie was a gap-toothed six year old with an open face and a winning smile. She was precociously bright and inquisitive. She wore her thick curly hair in pigtails. Peter was an intense, tiny, finely featured 5 year old.

Mr. Patel was an alert man, of East Indian origin in his 70's but weakened from a number of debilitating strokes. He had been the Minister of Health in the West Indian country that he came from and had been awarded an Order of the British Empire. He had his own room and spent much of his time in bed.

Mrs. Patel was a large, imposing woman, who worked weekends as a domestic in a hospital. She was recovering from a recent hysterectomy. She was outspoken and had strong opinions about people. She drank heavily. She was the most openly distraught over Violet's death: weeping, at times shrieking or wailing hysterically, and also expressing her fear and anger toward Mark.

I stayed at the apartment for hours, meeting with each person individually and also conferring with many of the family friends who were present. With the exception of Mr. Andrews and his wife, who were concerned and supportive toward the Patels, many of the friends would grill me about the "psychological dynamics" of the event, and expressed some sympathy towards Mark's position. By the end of the meetings, despite my own shock and sense of failure at having been unable to protect Violet, I had a clear sense that the Patels were prepared to care for the children and that the highest priority for the children was that they remain together, preferably with the Patels. There was one major problem: neither I nor the Patels had the authority to make that decision.

The Patels, lived in a different borough from the one where Violet had lived. The new borough assigned a social worker, Jen Nielson who was feeling overwhelmed by the situation and was finding her borough bureaucracy unsupportive. Her superiors did not want to take custody of the children and be encumbered with the obligations that this would entail. She already had a large caseload and did not yet have a personal connection with the family.

I, on the other hand, was concerned that my relationship with the family would cease. I felt that the family had begun to establish a relationship with me, based on my work with Violet. I also felt an overwhelming sense of obligation to help the children and the Patels, some of this emanating from my sense of guilt and inadequacy over Violet's death. I had been her social worker, she had warned me that this could happen, and it had.

Jen and I struck a deal. She would be the official representative of the state, the outside social worker, who would monitor the legal situation. I would be the inside social worker and provide counseling and advocacy. We would share the case management and meet regularly. We presented the plan to the family and they readily agreed. Our respective boroughs also supported the plan, and I received tremendous support from my supervisor, who recognized the importance of my continued involvement with the family for them and for me, despite the official termination of the borough's responsibility.

Jen and I also came to share an assumption that became a guiding principle in our work with the family: it was paramount for the children to remain together as a unit and not be placed separately in foster homes. They had in one violent act lost both of their parents, and they were adamant that they would not be separated. There were no foster homes that could take all of the children. There were two maternal uncles: one lived in the U.S. and had a large family of his own, and the other was a single man in his 20's; neither was in a position to care for the children. The family friends quickly drifted away, with the exception of the Andrews, and they could not take the children. This left the Patels.

The Patels were committed to caring for their grandchildren. The two generations, Violet's parents and her children, were bound together in their loss of her and maintained their continued relationship with her through each other. But there were enormous obstacles. The Patels were in poor health and at their age were not expecting to care for six children. Their flat was overcrowded. The four girls shared two beds in one room. Peter slept with Mr. Patel. Markie had to share a room with an elderly boarder, for whom Mrs. Patel was caring and with whom she had some kind of relationship. Within weeks, their landlord threatened them with eviction due to overcrowding.

There were other problems as well. Mr. and Mrs. Patel led parallel, separate lives and sometimes would denigrate one another in front of the children. Mrs. Patel would also accuse some of the children of having the "Johnson in them," particularly directing this at Markie, and to a lesser extent, Laura. She would also frequently harangue the children and was very preoccupied with her own needs. This was by no means an ideal situation, but all of us—Jen, the Patels, and the children—felt it was the best alternative available. An unspoken assumption, I believe, was that this was what Violet would have wanted as well.

It was not what Mark Johnson wanted, however. Although he was in prison, he technically had custody and wanted the children placed in foster homes rather than with the Patels. The borough was reluctant to assume the burden of taking custody of the children who were, therefore, made wards of the court, with supervision being given to the Patels. This gave the Patels limited financial resources to care for the children: Mr. Patel's pension, Mrs. Patel's meager wages, supplementary benefits for the children, and the income from the boarder. Eventually, after much advocacy and pressure, the Patel's borough took custody of the children 10 months after Violet's death, keeping them with their grandparents. More resources were then available, including a larger council house.

Jen and I visited Mr. Johnson in prison to discuss the situation with him. He struck me as an intelligent, charismatic man, who radiated an ineluctable destructiveness. He was furious about the arrangements and insisted that the children visit him. He refused to accept that the children did not want to visit him. He hated Mrs. Patel and blamed her for Violet's "provocative" behavior. He blamed me for Violet's death because I had never visited him and tried to help them work things out. He blamed Violet for her death because of the; "awful, untrue things she said about me in court." He blamed Jen for not forcing the children to see him.

Jen and I left the visit stunned and shaken. We reenacted this ordeal on a monthly basis as Mr. Johnson repeatedly demanded, through his lawyer, that the children visit him in prison. We patiently tried to explain why the children did not want to visit him and why we had placed them with the Patels. Jen and I were both relieved to have each other's company during these traumatizing encounters.

Mrs. Patel expressed fears to me, in front of the children, that Mr. Johnson would be released from prison and would kill her. There was also a family rumor that friends of Mr. Johnson might try and kidnap the children.

From the time of my first visit to the home, after Violet's death, I had worked out an intensive visiting schedule with the family at home and at the schools of the younger children. At the home visits I would see Mr. and Mrs. Patel individually and also meet with the three older girls as a group. The group meetings focused on shared reactions and ways that they could support themselves and their younger siblings. I would also touch base with the younger children at home. The family work involved a great deal of ventilation, clarification, and mediation. Obviously, grief work was a central theme in most of the sessions. But I also had to work on very concrete concerns with the grandparents, such as finances, the housing situation, the children's schoolwork. It was not possible to have the entire family sit together with me for sessions, and I did not try to push this. Rather, we would work in linked sub-units.

Much of my work with Mrs. Patel involved her grieving, but I also tried to mediate and buffer her destructive projections on to the children of her hatred of Mark. I, as well, had to confront her about her drinking and yelling at the children. With Mr. Patel, we developed a father and son type of relationship. I relied on him to provide consistent limits and support for the children despite the fact that he was frequently bed-ridden. He developed a deep relationship with Peter, and to a lesser extent, with Julie. They were often in his bedroom doing their home-work. I experienced him as a wise and gentle presence.

A great deal of conflict surfaced during my visits, usually between Mrs. Patel and the children. Tension would also erupt among the children. I would try to mediate but would leave each visit with at least one of the older girls not speaking to me. Fortunately, I managed to offend everyone more or less equally and was able to maintain my individual connections with all of the children.

Over time, the children began to use me in different ways and for different needs. Kate and Sandy would use me to share their feelings of loss, grief, and anger and would avidly seek out our individual sessions. Laura came less often and would sit more silently; when she did talk, she would describe more how she was coping than how she was griev-ing. Sandy developed a crush on me and would walk me to the bus stop at night when I would leave the home visits. In between visits she would write me notes, describing her sadness, how her stomach ached, and her fights with her friends. Once she described being punched in the stomach by a girl and retaliating violently because she said she felt like killing her. In her note she linked this to her memories of her mother's death. She signed it "Sandy—the beautifulest girl in the world—not really (I'm ugly)."

Julie and Peter would draw pictures for me, and we would tell stories to one another. I found them drawing pictures at home a week after Violet's death that depicted the murder. Julie's drawing showed stars where the death occurred and had pictures of her mother and a monster. Peter's picture was of the actual stabbing.

It is not possible or helpful to say who suffered the greatest loss when Violet died, but Markie's life changed dramatically. Violet was his main confidante, the person in the family who made the greatest effort to communicate with him. She would talk with him and read with him every day. Not only had he lost her, but he was now living in a chaotic situation, often overlooked, frequently confused, with one grandparent who feared him because he reminded her of her son-in-law and another grandparent who ignored him. The older girls were supportive of him, but they had their own adolescent lives to lead.

The school personnel were very cognizant of Markie's situation and made a special effort to be available to him. In addition, I would take him to professional soccer games on weekends and to karate classes during the week. For obvious reasons, it was important for Markie to feel as if he could defend himself. Although I spent more time with him than with any of the other children, I never felt as if I were reaching him in the same depth.

Two major rituals and events that punctuated our work were Violet's funeral and Mark's trial. Violet's body was badly damaged and the police needed to retain it for evidence for the murder trial. Although a memorial service was held shortly after Violet's death, there was a sense of unreality surrounding it and the children remained detached. Finally, five weeks after her death, Violet's body was released, and the funeral was held. The older girls were able to view the body before she was cremated. At the service, at first there was little visible reaction. Then Laura began to cry uncontrollably. As the grief slowly spread to all of the children, they all let go, wept without restraint, and bid Violet farewell.

Mark's murder trial was held in January, six months after Violet's death. Kate had to testify. This was traumatic for her, but she also felt as if she were contributing to justice on behalf of her mother. Mark was defiant and leered sexually at a woman, who sat next to me at the trial. However the trial was fairly straightforward, and Mark was found guilty and sentenced to life imprisonment. This seemed to be a source of relief for both the Patels and the children.

At night when I would leave the family, I would take a bus back to my bed-sit. The trip would take an hour and the bus would meander from one neighborhood to another, up High Street, down a church lane, through a dark, deserted common. The bus kept shifting direction but somehow it took me from their home to my own. I would sit on the second deck, passing their apartment (waving to Sandy at the window if she had not walked me to the bus stop) and think how the bus ride was a metaphor for my work with the family: not moving in a straight direction (at times appearing to be lost), but steadily moving on and connecting places and lives.

I realized that my life had become very intertwined with the Johnson children and their grandparents. I still was a recent immigrant to London. I had few friends, was involved in some unfulfilling affairs, and lived in a miserable, damp bed-sit, where I had to put shillings in my meter to get electricity and hot water. I was far away from my family. The Johnson children and the Patels, had become my family.

I was also stressed out. I had one record which I listened to over and over again, Marvin Gaye's *"What's Going On"*—"Mercy, Mercy,

Me," "Inner City Blues," "What's Going On," "Make Me Wanna Holler," and "Save the Children." I developed insomnia. When I did sleep I would have dreams about endangered pet birds that I would frantically and futilely try to save. My sister sent me a book about a baby gorilla at the Central Park Zoo that was separated from its mother and then reunited with her. When I read it, I found myself weeping uncontrollably, something that I had forgotten how to do. That night I dreamt about Julie losing her mother.

My supervisor was supportive but unable to provide clinical supervision, and I felt as if I could not afford to let my vulnerability show with her. Knowing that I needed clinical supervision and help with my counter-transference, I scheduled a meeting with a psychiatrist, who served as a consultant for the borough. In my one session with her, I found myself spending most of my energy trying to remain composed, as I outlined the situation. She was supportive of what I was doing and expressed concern about how it was affecting me, but I was too proud and well defended to respond to this. I did not see her again.

About a year and a half after I met Violet, I visited Ireland and fell in love with an Irish woman. I decided to move to Ireland. I rationalized to myself that the Johnsons and Patels were through the worst. Laura told me that I was abandoning them. I responded that they were stronger now and needed me less. What I didn't say, that was implicit in my actions, was that I had my own life to lead and that it was taking me away from them. Despite all of my rationalizations, I still felt deeply guilty about leaving them.

SEPARATION AND RE-CONNECTION

Jen remained as the family's social worker for a few months, but then she became pregnant and a new worker was assigned. After another few months, another worker was assigned. Social service reality was sinking in.

The children and I corresponded regularly. Kate and Sandy were particularly reliable letter writers, and both would use their letters as a continuation of our counseling sessions together, sharing profound feelings and current life dilemmas and struggles. Kate visited Mr. Johnson in prison once, on behalf of all of the children. She made it clear to him that none of the children ever wanted to see him again. They never did. Kate, Laura, and Sandy became involved with steady boyfriends.

My relationship did not work out. After 18 months, I was desperate to leave Ireland. I debated about whether I should return to the United States after three years abroad or go back to England. I ultimately decided to return to England, partially, although not exclusively, swayed by my concern for the Johnson children. I knew that I was no longer their social worker, but felt that our relationship was still important for all of us. A close relative in the United States questioned my professional boundaries. It was a fair question.

I returned to London and started a satisfying job for a family service agency in the same section of South London where I had previously worked. A few months after returning, I met my future wife and stepdaughter and moved in with them.

I remained in regular contact with the Johnsons and Patels but in a new role, as a family friend. Actually, I was more like a member of their extended family, like a close uncle or cousin. They would seek my advice about intimate concerns or mundane matters. They would feed me meals. I would have the kids over to my house for supper. They all came to my wedding. My stepdaughter and Julie attended the same summer day camp program that was run by the agency where I worked and where Kate was employed as a counselor.

After three years, my family and I decided to relocate to the United States. This felt less like an abandonment than had my previous departure for Ireland. Everyone in the Patel/ Johnson family seemed more settled, although Mr. Patel was not well and Laura (who was in a steady relationship) was pregnant. Still, everyone was moving on with their lives, in school or in jobs and with relationships, as was I. We were all still close, but less dependent on one another.

My wife and I held a going away party with our friends a few nights before we left London. The older children came with their boyfriends. It was an intimate and sad leave-taking. The morning that we were departing, and a couple of hours before leaving for the airport, I received a call from Kate, she had two things to tell me: Mr. Patel had died the day before, and the day before that, Laura had had her baby, a girl.

REFLECTIONS

Writing this story has been both painful and liberating. It is a story that I have carried around with me, for better or worse, for my entire career. For a few years after meeting the Johnsons, I was engaged in clinical work with very disengaged, disadvantaged families, and I threw myself into it. I had not learned to do clinical work in a more detached (professional?), self-protective way, and although the intensity of my involvement with the Johnsons, was never replicated, I would become very involved with the families with whom I worked. Partially, this was a function of my style, and it was also influenced by the agency that I worked for, which encouraged such intensity. It was no accident that I was working there. But this took its toll and I progressively worked my way into supervisory and administrative roles and eventually went on to do community organizing.

As my own family life developed, I realized that I would not have been able to do what I did with the Johnsons had I not been so alone at the time. Clearly, it meant a great deal for me to work so closely with them. They were a special family, and in our own ways we needed one another. I also think that, in some ways, we helped to heal one another. I hope so. I am painfully aware of the professional boundaries that I crossed in this work and still berate myself for things that I did or did not do.

Mark was in prison for seven years. Rumor has it that he remarried and has another family. Neither Mrs. Patel, the children, nor I regret not knowing for sure.

The three oldest girls are married to loving, gentle men. All three of them have children, six in all. Kate has worked for a multi-national corporation in a managerial capacity for many years. Laura and Sandy are devoted mothers. Julie became pregnant while in school and now has two children. She too has a stable relationship with a man and has been taking college courses in accounting. They all live within a few miles of each other in South London and remain in close contact.

Markie and Peter still live at home with Mrs. Patel. Peter has a steady job and a girlfriend and financially supports the family. Markie had been in a job training program for people with special needs, but the program was cut by the Thatcher government, and Markie has not worked or gone to school for years. His sisters are concerned that he uses drugs, but he denies it. Mrs. Patel is still alive. She is virtually blind after two cataract operations and drinks openly and regularly. Despite the difficult times that she has had with the children, she cared for them and she endured. They are devoted to her. She states that Markie is the most loyal of all of her grandchildren and is the one who takes care of her.

My family and I visit England every couple of years, and when we do, we always visit the Johnsons. We all get together in Mrs. Patel's council house, the same one that the children grew up in, and have what my wife has termed "a family reunion." My kids play with their kids. We cook food and reminisce, sharing memories of Violet and of our many experiences together. We joke about how Sandy used to "fancy" me. We take lots of group pictures. By the end, the sheer numbers of all of us in the tiny house become overwhelming, and we say tearful, hugging goodbyes.

We exchange Christmas cards and Kate and Sandy and I correspond, particularly after visits. Kate and her husband have visited us in the States.

I think of them at least every week, often more frequently. My thoughts are often tinged with regret and sadness, of ways that I let them down or didn't do enough. I worry about some of them. Sometimes I cry. I also feel a sense of pride about my work with them, as unorthodox as it was. I admire them. And of course I feel a deep sense of love and affection.

It strikes me as being ironic that I was Violet's social worker for only a few weeks and that I have loved her children, whom I know so much better than her, for over 20 years. And they still fondly think of me as their mom's social worker! And so, our chance meeting, that began as a professional encounter, in the Town Hall many years ago, changed all of our lives. And I am grateful for that.

POST SCRIPT

Since writing "Violet's Seeds," a great deal has happened, both between me and the children portrayed in the narrative, and within myself.

I mentioned the narrative to Sandy and to Kate in letters that I wrote to them, and Kate and I then became hooked up on e-mail. (We now correspond electronically at least once a week.) Kate conferred with two of her sisters, Laura and Sandy, and they asked to see the narrative. I initially felt some anxiety over this. Would it re-traumatize them to read it? Was I taking them on a journey that I was ready for but that they had not planned on? Would they like it? My wife reassured me that there was nothing in it about their mother's death that they did not already know and encouraged me to share it with them. Sonia Abels also urged me to do the same.

So with some trepidation I mailed them each a copy with a cover letter. I warned them of the painful content, explained why I felt the need to write it, predicted that some of my recollections might be faulty, and teased them about their aliases. I also suggested that they get together to discuss their reactions to it, which they agreed to do.

When they received their copies, they told Julie about what I had written, and she read the narrative as well. She was initially hurt that I had not sent her a copy of her own. The women also informed their brothers, who at this point asked not to read it (I am planning to contact them in the near future). We mutually made a decision, via e-mail, not to share it with Mrs. Patel, who might be upset by both the content and some of my comments about her.

I later learned that when Laura received the manuscript, she could not open it and telephoned Sandy. Sandy had been feeling sick with anticipation when the mail had been delivered the same morning and had initially resisted opening her copy. Sandy then read it to Laura over the phone. Kate e-mailed me, stating that they had all read and discussed it and that although they had many questions(why the title, why the names, why had I gotten certain facts wrong?) it had been a powerful yet positive experience for them. She also informed me that she was having Sandy and Julie and their children over for dinner on Sunday and that she was cooking them chili and banana bread, which is what I used to cook them when I would have them over for dinner.

So I phoned them on Sunday, and we had a very emotional, intimate conversation about the narrative and their reactions to it. I have since received lengthy letters from Sandy (who has also relayed Laura's reactions) and Julie. Kate, Sandy and Julie all have described how reading and talking about the tragedy has helped them to feel more connected with one another and that their private grief has moved to a shared bond of mutual loss and support. They had been in touch with their own reactions but had lost contact with what had happened to their siblings. Julie (who told me that she still has a "winning smile" but is no longer gap-toothed) described it as, "hanging on to our personal loss when it comes to Mum, instead of coming together and recognizing our collective loss." She was reminded of what it was like to have been six at the time, anguishing over her inability to protect Peter, who was free from the pain, now that she is revisiting those critical years from the perspective of a mother in her late 20's. Sandy shared how she had often wished that she were a boy, so that she could have protected her mother from her father. Kate has been reminded of the meaning of the scars that she carries on both of her hands from that fateful night.

Our letters and conversations have also focused on our relationships with one another. They have been struck by how young I was when I first met them. We have all let each other know how important we have been and still are to one another. The metaphor of "being like family" has been frequently invoked.

Sandy has been keeping her own journal, and Julie and Kate have some ideas for narratives of their own. We are corresponding regularly now, and I am encouraging them to write about what happened. I have described for them how I did not know what I was going to write or what I would learn from it until I actually wrote my piece. And I certainly did not know how it would re-invigorate our relationships and perhaps help them to explore their past and their deep attachments to one another together. Julie told me that what happened has always been a secret that she could not share with others, but that she now feels less inhibition about talking about it. It wasn't her fault; it was and is an important transformative part of her life, and some good things have even accrued from the tragedy. I appreciate her wisdom.

RETROSPECTIVE TO "VIOLET'S SEED" FIVE YEARS LATER

Re-reading "Violet's Seeds" five years later evoked deep emotions and responses. Imagining her death still feels like entering an icy chamber of despair and horror. Since writing the narrative I inhabit that place less often and can leave more easily. My continuing contact with Violet's survivors, her mother, six children and nine grandchildren is fulfilling and healing, moving the story forward, no longer a terrible moment frozen in time.

One way I think about the experience is to don my professional hat, and imagine it's happening to one of my students. I am immediately struck by the notion that the worker (the narrator) suffered what is known today as secondary trauma: the guilt, overwhelming emotions, rescue motifs, nightmares, social isolation, and persistent sadness, recognized as classic symptoms of a wounded helper. Secondary trauma was not a concept I was familiar with in the 1970's. It is a help-ful metaphor to put some things in perspective. At that time I was nei-ther in therapy nor receiving any clinical supervision to deal with my own feelings, reactions and counter-transference. Hopefully today, this is more readily available.

I have also re-examined the narrative to understand the develop-mental process of how the relationship moved from a strictly profes-sional relationship to what became a personal friendship, sometimes referred to as a "dual relationship." In the initial stage, Violet was my client and I provided support, resources, information, and some case management. During the second phase, immediately after her death, I provided crisis intervention to her children and parents. The third phase, the ongoing, clinical phase, was negotiated with the family, the social service department responsible for the children, and the social service department that employed me. In this phase I provided individ-ual counseling, family counseling, advocacy, brokering, mediation, and case management. A significant aspect of this phase is that I volun-teered, reflecting my desire to help, beyond the department's normal expectations. I believe this indicated my desire to help as a well-mean-ing professional and expressed my wish to make reparations to Violet's survivors and myself. It does suggest that *my needs*, were the motivat-ing factor in the desire to help this family. The intensity of the treatment to the children in my office, in their schools, and evenings in their home, led to an intimacy that sowed the seeds for the personal rela-tionship that succeeded the professional one. Was I the best person to provide those services? On the one hand I had credibility with the chil-dren and grandparents; I was Violet's social worker. On the other hand, I was emotionally wounded, and perhaps over-involved.

The next phase was the termination of my professional work with the family. This was not due to a cessation of need for further clinical services, but my own desire to pursue my life elsewhere.

The experience raises interesting dilemmas for social workers working with traumatized children in a deep and intense way. What kinds of time commitments should be made to such clients? Was it unethical that I left to meet my own needs, after having become so cen-tral to the family?

These troubling questions led me into the next phase, where I con-tinued my relationship with the family through correspondence. Pre-vailing professional wisdom suggests I should have ended the relationship. By staying actively in touch, it became a dual relationship. It is true that I was no longer their social worker, but what was our status as we corresponded: former social worker, family friend, quasi-relative? In a sense all three of these roles were realized as I returned to England, as the professional gave way to the personal. This continues to this day. Judging from letters received over the years from the now adult children and my own feelings, we relate very much as extended family.

If I was advising a student going through this: I would want them to get professional and personal help; urge them to think carefully about what they could offer the family and realistically commit to; and caution them against dual relationships. And yet, saying this still causes me ambivalence. I was 25 years old, and had worked with the family for 18 months, before and after Violet's tragic death. I saw the children multiple times each week, and also began to carry on my own personal life. I could not imagine how to just leave, both for their sake, which I was conscious of, and mine, which I was less conscious of.

The structure of the relationship changed. I moved from being their social worker, to a personal friendship.

Reflecting back, twenty-five years later, I do not think that I imagined that this relationship might endure for the rest of our lives. Was it harmful to them or helpful?

In July 2000, I had a reunion with the family, once again in Mrs. Patel's tiny council flat. All four of the "girls" (aged 40, 39, 37 and 30) were there, three of them with their husbands, with their collective brood of nine children, as well as my two teenage daughters. The "boys" were out. The husbands and children went down the block to the pub. Mrs. Patel lay in her bedroom with the door closed, the television on, drinking whisky as she always has. Kate, Laura, Sandy, Julie, and I were left alone in the living room where we reflected on our many years of knowing each other and how our lives remain intertwined. Sandy let me know that it had hurt her when I had neglected to send birthday cards for the past few years. We talked, as we always do, about their mother's death. Laura suddenly realized that at midnight it would be the 25th anniversary of the event, a fact that none of us had been conscious of when we had arranged our evening. There was silence, a collective shudder, some tears, and then we all held hands. Shortly after that the children and husbands re-entered and we all returned to our present lives, keenly aware of our shared pasts and our timeless bonds.

THE STORY OF LINDA AND PETER BIEHL: PRIVATE LOSS AND PUBLIC FORGIVENESS

9

By Peter and Linda Biehl

Peter and Linda Biehl,
the Amy Biehl Foundation.

Representing our daughter, Amy, we participated and gave testimony at the amnesty hearing for the four young men who murdered her. Recognizing the role of the Truth and Reconciliation Commission in South Africa's healing process, we did not oppose the Amnesty Committee's decision to grant them their freedom. We believe, as did our daughter, in the importance of democratic elections in South Africa. The amnesty hearings were but one condition in making them a reality. We grieve our loss, yet forgiveness has freed us. We can honor our daughter, we can remain true to her convictions, and we can carry on her work. Our narrative describes and explains our experience, the media and others' response to our decisions, and the meaning this has had to us and the members of our family: Kim, 31, Molly, 27, and Zach, 20.

PROLOGUE

We had expected the letter. From the day Amy's killers were sentenced to eighteen years in prison for murder and public violence, we had known amnesty applications were probable.

Still, the timing of the letter was interesting. Perhaps we search each event for the ironies, but the fax arrived from Cape Town on April 22nd: one day after Linda's birthday and four days before what might have been Amy's thirtieth. But irony was quickly lost in the plain reality of the words. Below is the letter-fax from the Amnesty Committee of South Africa's Truth and Reconciliation Commission.

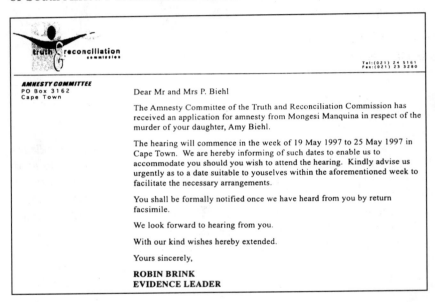

truth reconciliation
commission

Tel:(021) 24 5161
Fax:(021) 23 3280

AMNESTY COMMITTEE
PO Box 3162
Cape Town

Dear Mr and Mrs P. Biehl

The Amnesty Committee of the Truth and Reconciliation Commission has received an application for amnesty from Mongesi Manquina in respect of the murder of your daughter, Amy Biehl.

The hearing will commence in the week of 19 May 1997 to 25 May 1997 in Cape Town. We are hereby informing of such dates to enable us to accommodate you should you wish to attend the hearing. Kindly advise us urgently as to a date suitable to youselves within the aforementioned week to facilitate the necessary arrangements.

You shall be formally notified once we have heard from you by return facsimile.

We look forward to hearing from you.

With our kind wishes hereby extended.

Yours sincerely,

ROBIN BRINK
EVIDENCE LEADER

We knew Manquina's application would be joined by the other three. That was a foregone conclusion. But the others had until May 10, 1997, in which to apply. That was the official cut-off date for amnesty applications.

We were advised by John Allen of Archbishop Tutu's office that the four applicants would present themselves in a single hearing. Given the immediate proximity of the proposed May 19th hearing week, counsel for the applicants could easily appear and request a postponement to provide adequate preparation time. We could make a very long and expensive trip for nothing. This seemed unreasonable and unfair.

Upon consideration of our request that the hearing be re-scheduled to coincide with our planned visit to Cape Town in late June and July, the Amnesty Committee agreed to re-set the hearing, for July 8–9, 1997. We were thankful to be spared the expense and probable frustration of an early trip and were grateful for some additional time in which to prepare our statement for the hearing.

There was no question of our participation in the hearing. Amy had informed us four years earlier that the Truth and Reconciliation process was a key pre-negotiated condition upon which free elections for all South Africans could be granted by the National Party—in power at the time. More importantly, a procedure for granting of amnesty in forgiveness of politically directed crimes was essential to the pro-apartheid regime before it could open the ballot boxes to the certainty of Black majority rule.

Amy had said that Nelson Mandela and his African National Congress (ANC) colleagues had refused to accept a blanket amnesty provision and had compromised on case-by-case amnesty, earned on the merits of the evidence presented, against a rigorous standard for proof.

Given this background insight and Amy's passionate efforts to gain free and democratic elections for all South Africans, we could not ignore the Amnesty Committee process. Our failure to appear and participate in the hearing could be interpreted as displaying a lack of respect for a healing process, honorably negotiated and now publicly and unequivocally championed by President Mandella, Archbishop Tutu and other respected South Africans.

We knew we must participate in the process and, believing in it, that we could not oppose amnesty if it were granted on the merits. We were certain Amy would concur.

News of the hearing schedule spread quickly. So did our indication to the Amnesty Committee that we would not retain legal counsel or oppose amnesty, if granted.

Media representatives from South Africa and throughout the United States began telephoning us with their inevitable inquiries. On a small scale, it was reminiscent of the media blitz in the early hours and days following Amy's death.

Always, the questions: ". . . but, aren't you angry?" or ". . . you mean you are prepared to forgive your daughter's killers?" It reminded Linda of the days in 1993 when producers from the television tabloid news "magazines" and popular "talk" shows would telephone her looking for an indication that she might like to appear on camera and get "mad." Linda was always so calm, rational, and unsensational that the producers or "talent" people never called back.

Once again, we succeeded in boring the reporters with our peaceful resolve in our decision not to oppose the amnesty applications from Amy's killers. Generally, the reporters were not equipped with backgrounds which would enable them to understand our position. So they covered the story and went on to the next one.

The *Houston Chronicle,* however, sent South African reporter Tony Freemantle, who had written an award-winning feature piece on truth commissions in 1996. Tony spent an entire day with us in our home. He understood our attitude and the basis for it—although he conceded that he might not be capable of it, himself. His front-page piece for the *Chronicle* ran on Sunday, May 11th—one day after the cut-off date for amnesty applications to South Africa's Truth and Reconciliation Commission. It was also Mother's Day (irony again), but Linda didn't seem to notice.

Freemantle's piece was informed and insightful. People told us they found it helpful in understanding our position because it was placed in a well-researched context. This is testimony to the utility of good journalism.

Our preparation for Cape Town really centered around our desire to arrange a meaningful experience for the Kendall family of St. Louis, who would be traveling with us for the first ten days of the trip. The Kendalls have become very important in the educational outreach activities of the Amy Biehl Foundation in the United States and—on their first visit to South Africa—we wanted them to experience vividly the joys and sorrows of life in the townships and informal settlements, to see the contrast with Cape Town's beaches and riches. We wanted them to see what Amy saw. Moreover, as friends, we wanted them to see some of the work we are doing in the Western Cape and to meet some of the people and organizations who are contributing to the building of the new South Africa.

We kept telling ourselves that we would prepare a written statement for presentation at the amnesty hearing. We wanted to be certain of our word choice. Every word must be just right.

Former Ambassador, Princeton Lyman, who had officially informed Linda of Amy's death from Pretoria in 1993, volunteered to review and comment on our prepared statement before our departure. He never had the opportunity to be of service.

When we boarded our flight on June 26, we had no written statement.

We knew our feelings—what was in our hearts and in our heads.

In so many ways, we had been prepared for this event. For years, we had taken our kids to Sunday school. For years, we had taught Sunday school classes in Christian ethics. Standing at the kitchen telephone, moments after learning of Amy's death, Linda recalls fielding a constant stream of telephone calls and visitors thinking the words, "Father, forgive them, for they know not what they do."

While we have never been serious readers of the Bible, few words could be more appropriate in considering the circumstances of Amy's death. Her friends tried to tell Amy's killers that she was a "comrade" in their struggle. But try reasoning with an angry mob in the heat of battle. It was too late. Amy's killers saw only a white person.

Amy had prepared us for this. On the subject of Black violence against White South Africans, Amy repeatedly admonished us to remember that the frustrated and angry Black youth ". . . are only doing what has been done to them by generations of White oppressors."

Moreover, Amy's admonition that ". . . when Black South Africans die in the struggle, only numbers are reported—but when White people die, they get complete obituaries with names, families, pets, and everything," was ringing in our ears.

Her dismay at this indignity had been prophetic in the case of her own death in South Africa's struggle. We knew how Amy would feel about the media blitz which had followed her death. After all, she had confided to friends that—in the event of her death—she wanted the same impersonal press treatment accorded her Black colleagues in the struggle.

So . . . prepared by our own personal background experiences and by our daughter's words in the years and days before her death, there were never any questions about our position. It was a time for humility—a time for forgiveness.

In the end, we knew the words would come. So, armed with Amy's words and a few related materials, we departed for Cape Town.

We were not expecting the international media attention which greeted our arrival in Cape Town. There were television cameras and newspaper reporters present when we entered the international passenger terminal at the airport. While loading our luggage into a van, a man approached to say, simply, ". . . I am a resident of Cape Town and I want to thank you for what you are doing."

Within minutes of arrival in our hotel room, the telephone rang. It was a reporter for the *London Times* in the hotel lobby and requesting an interview—on the spot, if we didn't mind. We hadn't begun to unpack our bags.

Everywhere we went in Cape Town, the reporters followed us. It was the pending Amnesty Committee hearing that was fueling their engines. More than this, however, it was the fact that we were not opposing the amnesty applications which was the "story."

It was interesting to us that our acceptance of South Africa's truth and reconciliation process should be so curious—so "newsworthy." What should be so strange about this in a country where reconciliation and forgiveness is national policy, rooted in centuries of southern African tradition?

Befitting the almost-comic character of all of this media attention, during a rooftop interview on July 7 for live broadcast to the U.S. for CBS television's morning news, Linda's answer to the first question posed to us was suddenly interrupted when some unknown technician introduced an Afrikaans cartoon show on-air in our place. The producer's shouting through our earphones from New York did nothing to restore our live hook-up. A $20,000 satellite booking was, therefore, unceremoniously ended.

We found ourselves wondering why a major news network would go through so much effort and expense to ask us why we would not oppose four amnesty applications in a hearing room the following morning.

On the morning of July 8, we were met at the hotel by our Amnesty Committee Briefer, Paul Haupt. A very professional young psychologist, Paul was assigned to us to be certain we understood the process, to help us anticipate the graphic testimony which would be given with respect to Amy's murder, and to ensure that we were holding up under the pressure.

Our calm seemed to surprise Haupt and—more than once—we teased him with offers to serve as his Briefer. He accompanied us as we walked the few blocks to the Amnesty Committee's hearing room— surrounded, as we walked, by television camera and sound crews.

The press of reporters on the sidewalk at 106 Adderty Street was fierce as we passed through lobby security and entered an elevator. We were fairly certain the reporters and camera crews would pin us against elevator walls and trample us.

Through it all, we kept our focus and assured the press that we would do our communicating in the hearing room and at a press conference when the hearing had concluded. During that elevator ride to the Amnesty Committee offices, I felt Amy was close to us—understanding what we were experiencing and encouraging us to rise to the occasion.

In the months and years since Amy's death, we have reflected from time to time on the adage which suggests that ". . . a child shall lead you," and we can only say that our daughter has led us through some very challenging times—growing into young adulthood and, now, in a country half way around the world. But—in the midst of the lights, cameras, microphones, questions, jostling, and noise—we knew precisely where we were going and why we were there. Amy had prepared us well for this experience. Now . . . if we could just hold up our end of the equation.

The quiet of the judge's offices near the hearing room was welcome and we could see the three judges and two lawyers who comprised the Amnesty Committee wolfing down some tea and pastries during the recess which preceded our hearing. With a backlog of more than 5000 cases and an entire nation of hearing rooms to reach, these judges must have precious little time in life's small pleasures and many miles between sleeps.

The quiet freeze-frame was broken by a small and silent procession of eight figures who appeared suddenly in the corridor leading to the hearing room. In an instant, we shared a narrow hallway with four inconspicuously armed security men... and with four of Amy's killers.

They were in street clothes. No handcuffs. They appeared a bit uneasy and surprised to encounter us. It was my first time encountering them. Linda had already experienced the Supreme Court trial and had watched three of them carefully on several occasions.

I was within inches of my daughter's killers and—somehow—I was in control of my emotions. In retrospect, I know Amy's hand was on my shoulder at that moment. Linda has said that she doesn't feel anger when she sees Amy's killers, only a sort of profound sadness—a void. I know now what she means. She has described the feeling exactly.

Media representatives were permitted in the crowded hearing room for fifteen minutes before we entered. The families of the four applicants were brought to us in a steady stream—one after another. "We're parents too . . ." we said to them. We wanted the parents to know that we could understand a bit of what they might be thinking and that if their sons should be fortunate enough to win amnesty, we expected them to be responsible parents and to be accountable for the behavior of their sons. Accountability is an important aspect of forgiveness. Amnesty demands accountability in order to establish balance and equity in the equation.

The statements of the four amnesty applicants were read into the record by their two attorneys—retained as counsel by the Pan African Congress (PAC) on whose behalf the applicants claimed to be acting when they attacked Amy. The statements were carefully prepared to meet the tests for amnesty: a political motive was established for the murder, a confession was made to the act of murder, and an apology was offered to Amy's parents and family.

To hear these statements read into the record by attorneys—rather than by the applicants established distance between the applicants and us, even though they were seated barely ten feet away.

For me, it created an almost abstract quality to the statements. Although they were quite graphic in their recounting of the act, and although the words tore at me inside, I felt somehow removed and empty of emotion.

By contrast, the statements were very real to the parents and families of the applicants. At least one parent left the room when her son's confession to stabbing Amy in the heart was read. The four applicants had denied participation in Amy's murder during their Supreme Court trial. I am certain that parents were hoping—somehow—that words of confession would not have to be spoken. Hearing the words must have been very difficult.

I believe the experience in the hearing room must have been more difficult for the applicants' parents than for us. We felt liberated in our position and free from guilt. We were confident that we were completely consistent with Amy's expectations of us.

We had spent part of a day in our hotel room drafting our statement. It came naturally and—in the end—it was really a matter of who would deliver which portions. It seemed right that Linda, as Amy's mother and the one most responsible for her character development, should present Amy to those in the hearing room, and I would articulate our support of the truth and reconciliation process and our rationale for not opposing amnesty.

STATEMENT BY PETER BIEHL

"Thank you Mr. Chairman, members of the Amnesty Committee, for taking a few moments to hear our statement.

We come to South Africa as Amy came, in a spirit of committed friendship, and, make no mistake about it, extending a hand of friendship in a society which has been systematically polarized for decades is hard work at times. But Amy was always about friendship, about getting along, about the collective strength of caring individuals and their ability to pull together to make a difference, even to transform corrupt nation states.

In her valedictory high school graduation speech in 1985, Amy quoted biologist Lewis Thomas on the importance of collective thinking. Thomas said:

> "The drive to be useful is encoded in our genes, but when we gather in very large numbers, as in the modern nation state, we seem capable of levels of folly and self-destruction to be found nowhere else in all of nature."

But he continues,

> ". . . if we keep at it and keep alive we are in for one surprise after another. We can build structures for human society never seen before, thoughts never thought before, music never heard before."

This was Amy at age 18. This was Amy on the day she died. She wanted South Africans to join hands to sing music never heard before, and she knew this would be a difficult journey.

On 21 June 1993, just two months before she died, Amy wrote in a letter to the *Cape Times* Editor:

> "Racism in South Africa has been a painful experience for Blacks and Whites and reconciliation may be equally painful. However, the most important vehicle toward reconciliation is open and honest dialogue."

Amy would have embraced your truth and reconciliation process. We are present this morning to honour it and to offer our sincere friendship. We are all here in a sense to consider and to value a committed human life which was taken without opportunity for dialogue. When this process is concluded we must link arms and move forward together.

Who, then, is Amy Biehl? Amy was one of our four children. Her sisters are Kim, who is now 31, Molly 27, and her brother Zach, aged 20. We are very proud of all of our children and their accomplishments. But because Amy was killed in South Africa, because our lives have now become forever linked to South Africa, we are here to share a little of Amy with you.

Amy was a bright, attractive child. She loved competitive sports such as swimming, diving, gymnastics, among others. She played the flute, the guitar. She studied ballet. She was a focused student from the very beginning, always striving for straight A's. I'm going to read a page from Amy's high school journal so in her own words you can get a glimpse of her. This is Monday, October 3rd, 1983. She was 16.

> "I have had more homework this year than I have ever had before. In lots of ways this has helped me because I have been forced to get organized and really dig in. But I have also been forced to stay up until 11:30 or 12:00 each night making me very cranky during the day. One thing that worries me is whether or not I will be able to keep this rigorous schedule up and still keep straight As. Every night after school I have some activity to attend be it diving, band, flute or something else and starting in November I'll be swimming every day. I hate it when people say you should cut down your schedule, you're too busy, because I have already cut out several other activities. I'm kind of addicted to exercise and get very bored if I am not constantly busy. School is very important to me but being active and well-rounded are necessary for me to be happy. I want to have a 4.0 but I also want to be an award-winning drum major, first chair flute, a State champion diver, as far as I am concerned why can't I. I think I will be able to make it through this year. I am a very hard worker at everything I do, and as long as I know what I want I can get it. Besides, getting a 90% on a Chemistry test makes staying up all night worth it".

Upon high school graduation she went to Stanford University. It was her dream to do that. At Stanford she evolved as a serious student and she began to focus her academic work on the Southern Africa region. Her love of Nelson Mandela as a symbol of what was happening in South Africa grew.

After her 1989 Stanford graduation she made her first trip to Africa. I am going to read the Statement of Purpose she compiled for her Ph.D. programme to bring her forward to August 1993. And she wrote this the summer of 1993 shortly before her murder.

STATEMENT OF PURPOSE—AMY BIEHL

My purpose in applying for graduate study is to complete a Ph.D. in Political Science. Within the field I intend to focus on recent democratic transitions in Southern Africa building on my previous research and practical working experience in this area.

In September 1989 1 received a degree in International Relations emphasizing Third World development and Africa from Stanford University.

I completed a departmental Honours thesis on American Foreign Policy in South Africa entitled, "Chester Crocker and the Negotiations for Namibian Independence: the role of the individual in recent American Foreign Policy."

In May 1989, 1 subsequently received a Bowman Undergraduate scholarship to continue my research in Namibia from July to September 1989. My paper assessing the pre-election environment in Namibia was subsequently used at Stanford in its Modem African History course.

In September 1990, after a year of work for a Democratic Congressman on Capitol Hill, I began work at the Washington-based National Democratic Institute for International Affairs, NDI. NDI represents the Democratic Party internationally and conducts political development programmes in emerging democracies. With NDI, I worked in Namibia, South Africa, Burundi, Congo, Giyana, Surinam, and Zambia along with former President Jimmy Carter.

I wrote briefing papers on six African countries for Democratic Party chairman Ron Brown and coordinated a visit by the Prime Minister of Namibia to the 1992 Democratic National Convention. I also wrote an article on NDI's approach to democratization in Africa published in an international journal.

Based on my undergraduate research experience and my work at NDI, I developed a proposal to research the participation of women in South Africa's transition for which I received a 1992/93 Fulbright Scholarship.

I am currently based in Cape Town affiliated with the Community Law Centre at the University of the Western Cape, directed by Advocate Abdullah Omar.

I am working with Bridget Mabandla, senior researcher at the Community Law Centre. At the Community Law Centre I have undertaken the following projects: researching comparative structures for women in decision-making, analyzing the constitutional proposals and technical committee reports currently being debated with regard to women and gender; locating women with various political organizations and coalitions, and assessing the impact of women within these organizations with respect to evolving transitional structures.

I have written an occasional paper for the Community Law Centre focusing on structure for women in political decision-making, and a chapter on women in the transition for an upcoming book to be published in the United States. I have co-authored articles published in the Weekly Mail, the Argus, Democracy in Action and Femina. At the completion of my grant, I will present a paper entitled Women in a Democratic South Africa: from Transition to Transformation.

I could go on but this was basically what she was doing, and what she intended to do was to pursue a Ph.D. in Political Science, to teach and study about politics and particularly African politics.

Who is Amy to South Africa and what is her legacy here?

Linda and I were struck by photos which appeared immediately after Amy's death in the *Los Angeles Times* and other newspapers around the world which showed Amy as a freedom fighter, and in subsequently reading President Mandela's autobiography, *A Long Walk to Freedom,* and determining how President Mandela and his colleagues value the role of freedom fighting. We were struck when on June 1st, 1996, in Los Angeles, California, at a dinner to honour Chinese dissidents and freedom fighters from Tianamen Square, Amy was presented the Spirit of Tianamen Square Award, posthumously, for her reputation and track record as a freedom fighter in many countries on the continent of Africa.

We think in view of the importance of freedom fighting in our world, this is a precious legacy of Amy for us. We think Amy's legacy in South Africa, additionally, is as a catalyst and perhaps her death represented a turning point in things in this country with specific regard to the violence which was occurring at the time.

We received literally hundreds of letters from South African citizens and I would read you just briefly from one which had to do with Amy as a catalyst in terms of the violence at the time.

This is from an Eric van Vyver of George, South Africa:

"Dear Mr and Mrs Biehl

Sometimes during one's lifetime something happens which is so unbelievably terrible and so very, very sad that one is left without words to convey the deep sympathy felt for family and loved ones. Your daughter's death has left millions of my country-people feeling this way.

> I am, however, completely convinced that August 25th 1993 will always be remembered as the day on which South Africa came to realize that we are leaning into an abyss of total self-destruction. Then Amy died and an entire nation took a step back. I hope and know that this will comfort you and please believe that what I am saying is true."

Amy's legacy is also as an advocate of human rights, an empowerer of women and children. Our beautiful women of Mosaic who are seated here today and yesterday are tangible evidence of Amy's legacy in South Africa. These women of courage work round the clock every day in the townships and informal settlements empowering and counseling women and children and enabling them to assume roles in the prevention of violence in their communities. Linda and I are very proud of Mosaic and we can think of no more beautiful evidence of Amy's continuing legacy in your beautiful country.

Additionally, Amy's friend and colleague, Rhoda Kadalie, has now assumed the post, an important post in the Human Rights Commission. Amy would be very proud of that and very proud of Rhoda's and the Commission's continuing work to preserve human rights.

I will read to you briefly from a letter we received from Minister Dullah Omar dated on the 25th of August 1993:

> "Everyone who knew Amy will bear witness that she worked untiringly in the gender research project to ensure that the issue of women's rights was prioritized on the agenda for a political settlement in South Africa. She was thus also highly regarded by all her colleagues and peers, both in Cape Town and indeed everywhere in the country for her diligence and commitment to the issue of women's rights.
>
> We want to say to you that your beloved Amy became one of us in her spirited commitment to justice and reconciliation in South Africa. Amy's passing is not just a loss to the Community Law Centre, or University community, it is a loss for all committed democrats in this country.
>
> Despite the fact that Amy was often very busy, she managed to prepare a briefing paper or two for me. This is how I got to know Amy, always willing to help. I will therefore personally miss her a great deal."

Finally, Amy's legacy to South Africa is as a friend. I will read just quickly from a letter we received dated August 27, 1993, from Randy Erentzen at the Centre for Development Studies.

> "When Amy left my office on Wednesday she said to me, "Hey, if I don't see you, thanks for everything." The next time I saw her I

was removing her jewelry from her dead body. I shuddered for a moment as I put the blood-stained bangles and rings into my pocket and I thanked her silently for being my friend.

I write to thank you and the rest of your family for giving Amy to us. I want you to know that she was a most sensitive and wonderful human being.

When I first encouraged her to come to South Africa to study and when I wrote the recommendations for Amy to receive the Fulbright Scholarship, and when I introduced her to my colleagues at the University, I knew I was doing so for somebody I really believed in.

Together we traveled through South Africa helping to prepare our people for the country's first ever democratic elections. She danced with us late at night in the townships. Amy was so full of the rhythm of life. She danced better than many Africans and was greatly envied for her ability to imbibe so much of the culture, traditions and history of our people. Amy's death has brought home once again the potential beauty of this country to which she eventually gave her life.

Now, in closing, a few comments. We have the highest respect for your Truth and Reconciliation Commission process. We recognize that if this process had not been a pre-negotiated condition, your democratic free elections could not possibly have occurred. Therefore, and believing as Amy did in the absolute importance of those democratic elections occurring, we unabashedly support the process which we recognize to be unprecedented in contemporary human history.

At the same time, we say to you that it's your process, not ours. We cannot, therefore, oppose amnesty if it is granted on the merits. In the truest sense it is for the community of South Africa to forgive its own and this has its basis in traditions of ubuntu and other principles of human dignity. Amnesty is clearly not for Linda and Peter Biehl to grant.

You face a challenging and extraordinarily difficult decision. How do you value a committed life? What value do you place on Amy and her legacy in South Africa? How do you exercise responsibility to the community in granting forgiveness in the granting of amnesty? How are we preparing prisoners, such as these young men before us, to re-enter the community as a benefit to the community, acknowledging that the vast majority of South Africa's prisoners are under 30 years of age? Acknowledging as we do that there's massive unemployment in the marginalized community; acknowledging that the recidivism rate is roughly 95%. So how do we, as friends, link arms and do something?

There are clear needs for prisoner rehabilitation in our country as well as here. There are clear needs for literacy training and education, and there are clear needs for the development of targeted job skill training. We, as the Amy Biehl Foundation, are willing to do our part as catalysts for social progress. All anyone need do is ask.

Are you, the community of South Africa, prepared to do your part? In her 21 June 1993 letter to the *Cape Times* editor, Amy quoted the closing lines of a poem, "Victoria West," written by one of your local poets. We would close our statement with these incredible words:

"They told their story to the children. They taught their vows to the children, that we shall never do to them what they did to us."

Thank you for listening.

* * *

When we finished our presentation, Linda and I knew we had done the right thing. We had remembered Amy and her dreams for South Africa. We had spoken for her, in her absence, and we could hold our heads up and move on with life.

EPILOGUE

The call came at 1:00 in the morning. Tuesday, July 28, 1998. We had been home from Cape Town only one day.

Amnesty had been announced. It was 10:00 a.m. in Cape Town and Amy's four killers were walking from their prisons into the embraces of family and friends. While we were still on the telephone, our fax whirred to life and the Amnesty Committee's official pronouncement began to appear.

When we hung up the telephone, we were suddenly missing Amy very much. By 1:30 a.m., telephone calls were coming in from South Africa's media. At 7:30 that evening, we closed our door behind the last American television crew. At some part in that long and frenetic day, we telephoned our children to inform and prepare them.

The next morning, a CNN live telephone interview at 6:25—and within an hour, on a flight from Palm Springs to New York for Thursday morning's "GOOD MORNING AMERICA" interview. That day, our voice mail collected 34 messages—most of them from media representatives and producers. That night, Linda and I walked the streets of New York and found a small, friendly French restaurant we remembered.

We were tired, but we were at peace with ourselves. We slept soundly—if briefly that night.

Many people have expressed disbelief and "amazement" at our support for the truth and reconciliation process and at our forgiving attitude.

To us, forgiveness is opening the door to a full and productive life. We can honor Amy, can be true to her convictions, and can carry on with her work and with ours. Forgiving is liberating. By contrast, it seems to us that hatred consumes tremendous energy—negative energy—and robs people of their productivity. Hatred, in the end, is a totally selfish behavior.

The real burden in forgiveness falls to those who are forgiven and to those who are closest to them. Our statement—released to the press on the morning amnesty was announced—speaks to this point, among others.

STATEMENT BY LINDA AND PETER BIEHL:

Amy was drawn to South Africa as a student and she admired the vision of Nelson Mandela of a "Rainbow Nation." It is this vision of forgiveness and reconciliation that we have honored.

As Amy's parents, we have worked with and learned about many South Africans. We have shared South Africa's pain. We must never forget people who lost their lives in the struggle. We must honor them in discovering new approaches—nonviolent partnerships—to create the South Africa with Nelson Mandela that Amy and those who perished dreamed of—a new, multi-racial, democratic nation.

We are concerned, therefore, about the violence which still exists and which surely will escalate as the 1999 elections approach. Amy was one of many killed in the violent political climate preceding the 1994 elections. Unfortunately, we are seeing today similar power struggles occurring throughout communities and the country. Violence remains the order of the day in promoting certain political agendas. Violence and fear are never hallmarks of a democratic way of life.

We are keenly aware, as we work with people of disadvantaged communities, of the need for change in the lives of South Africa's marginalized people. We have experienced our own small struggles in trying to complete projects in partnership with many community groups. Obstacles abound. Community requests are made, partnerships are formed, but implementation is slow. Regardless of the roadblocks or the minefields, we shall continue, within our limits, to work in partnership with people who are wonderfully inspired to help themselves. We are working on violence prevention projects throughout the Cape Flats and hope to encourage and motivate other people to do the same thing. We have enjoyed many positive experiences with great partners and highly recommend this type of service to South Africa.

It is important to stress that *every* life is significant. Amy's life and death received much publicity. As Amy's parents, we have experienced great pain—but we are not alone. Working through the pain has not been easy, but we have learned so much about South Africa's pain while on our personal journey.

The amnesty process has been a unique experience for individuals and for South Africa as a nation. Decisions made are not to be taken lightly. If amnesty is granted to individuals who have been imprisoned, it is essential for families and communities to support these individuals upon their release. In the cases of the four amnesty applicants in Amy's murder, we hope they will receive the support necessary to live productive lives in a non-violent atmosphere. In fact, we hope the spirits of Amy and of those like her will be a force in their new lives.

Again, we encourage all stakeholders to accelerate their pace toward cooperation; to be instruments of change in the marginalized communities; to advance holistic approaches to violence reduction and prevention.

We thank those partners who have helped and supported us thus far, and we pledge to work hard with the South African people to continue the all-important nation-building process. We will do all we can to help fulfill the vision of your free, rainbow nation—a vision which Amy shared with you.

We have been asked repeatedly whether the amnesty process has brought us "closure." We reply that we have never sought closure and have no desire to close the book on Amy.

The Chilean playwright/poet/human rights activist, Ariel Dorfman, responded profoundly to our question on closure in Cape Town in July, 1997:

> I think closure happens when you have the body. When the person who hurt that body asks for forgiveness, repents for having done that and says they will not do it again. That is a form of closure. I think . . . I think . . . closure happens that because those

bodies disappeared or were hurt because of all the damage done, the results rather than being held are a step towards paradise. In the sense that though every death is terrible, a death in vain is much more terrible than a death that led to a community resolving its problems. I would say closure particularly happens when every person in that community is able to take that person home with them and make that person part of their home and part of their lives.

On the other hand, I feel we should not lie about closure—we should not see closure for its own sake or seek closure as the solution to all problems. Because I do believe there are pains we should not pretend do not exist. I'm sorry to put this as bluntly as I am doing, but even all the closure in the world cannot return Amy Biehl. I mourn for it, I grieve for it. I do think we have to deal with the ambiguity of existence. It is difficult to deal with. The Truth and Reconciliation Committee is being asked to deal with all those things—it is being asked to do more than it can possibly do. It cannot offer closure. Each person will find his own form of closure. Closure is satisfactory—it's a haven—but closure also means to close, and close is the opposite of life. Life opens. So, at times we have to live with those wounds and those openings and there is no alternative because we cannot save the basic mystery of life. And that life is entangled with death in a tremendous way.

To which we reply, "AMEN!"

APPENDIX
ETHICS STUDY GUIDE
AND ACTIVITIES

THE NARRATIVE

In narrative or story form describe an ethical problem you faced in your professional practice while working with persons in families, groups, individuals, communities, organizations, institutions, programs, and policy development. Use the story to provide the context surrounding the ethics problem and how you have experienced it.

THE PROCESS

1. Describe the ethical problem with which you are concerned as thoroughly and accurately as possible. Examples include:

   • Sharing information about an adolescent with his/her family without the youth's permission

- Violating an agency's policy
- Carrying out an agency policy that you believe will harm clients
- Maintaining a "friendship relationship" with a family after service was terminated
- Using a practice approach defined by the agency which you know (from your own experience and research) is unsuccessful
- Informing authorities about a client's action without his/her knowledge
- Assigning a higher grade than the student's work reflects
- Supporting the children of a dying parent to encourage the doctor to permit euthanasia
- Recommending to a lesbian that she terminate her three month pregnancy
- Providing therapy on the Internet
- Engagement in an aspect of genetic counseling.

2. Formulate a hypothesis that you believe best defines the issue you are working on and that shifts the problem toward a solution. A couple of examples are:

- It should be the case that the adolescent be asked to tell his/her own parents about his/her own actions
- It should be the case that the worker violates the agency's policy of harm and informs the agency of what the client is doing and the reasons for the action.

3. Indicate the conflicting aspects of the ethical problem. Describe the process you used to make the decision, including supporting data: research, professional knowledge, other professionals, clients, and other such resources.

THE DECISION

Questions to be addressed:

1. How would you check to see that, if acted upon, your decision was right?
2. If the decision were a mistake, what might indicate this?

3. What other information could have been collected to make a better, more grounded decision?
4. What are the alternatives to the decision you made? Rank the alternatives from the most to least viable.
5. Who could make a better decision and why?
6. Who might disagree with your decision and why?
7. Is there any principle in your professional code that supports your decision?
8. How do you think your ethical decision contributes to the good of the society?

INDEX